Well
I Never Knew That!

John Parker

Edward Gaskell *publishers*
DEVON

First published 2008
Edward Gaskell *publishers*
The Old *Gazette* Building
6 Grenville Street
Bideford
Devon
EX39 2EA

isbn(10) 1-906769-02-8
    (13) 978-1906769-02-4

Well, I Never Knew That!

John Parker

Typeset, printed and bound by
Lazarus Press
Caddsdown Business Park
Bideford
Devon
EX39 3DX
www.lazaruspress.com

This book is dedicated to my late, dear wife Jeanne, who passed away on Christmas day 1999; who supported me in all my maritime endeavours, when we were both involved with the *Cutty Sark* Tall-Ships' festivals around our coast, during the 1980s and the 1990s, giving me the inspiration and incentive to research, and to write this lexicon for the furtherence and understanding of our maritime language

Why is a ship called She?
(From an old china mug)

A ship is called 'She' because
There is always a great deal of bustle about her.
There is usually a gang of men about,
She has a waist and stays;
And it takes a lot of paint to keep her looking good.
It is not the initial expence that breaks you,
It is the upkeep.
She can be all decked out,
but it takes an experienced man to handle her correctly.
Without a man at the helm,
she is absolutely uncontrollable.
She shows her topsides,
and hides her bottom,
And when coming in to port
she always heads for the bouys.

Illustrations

Introduction

This publication has taken much research, not only from the information found in reference books, which accounts for about one third of the content, but from sources collected over many years, during my past as a 'Closet Seaman': conversations with maritime folk, with crews of the 'Tall ships' in and around the United Kingdom. By listening to the tales of 'Old Salts', and those working with wooden and metal-hulled ships in this country and abroad. All these experiences, plus watching and questioning, have brought about the larger portion of this book.

The United Kingdom being a group of countries surrounded by sea, has the majority of our countrymen living around the coast, and most others no more than a couple of hours from the sea and its ports; so great numbers of people have, or have had, family with strong links to the sea. It is little wonder that our maritime history has had such an influence on the English language, with its words and expressions being passed down through the centuries, by our maritime ancestors, and is still in common use today.

There are a good number of books in which we can find general naval-terms, but I have yet to find one that gives exclusively to words, terms, clichés, that we still use in our everyday language.

To many of these explanations, research has thrown up varying translations. Some will have been lost in the mists of time, some, I believe to be speculation; to these, I have drawn my own conclusions and given you what I think to be correct. However, in these instances the reader has the prerogative to take whichever they deem to be right. No one can say for certain that every word and explanation, given by anyone on this subject, is absolutely correct, especially when one considers that most sailors, below deck, in years gone by, were illiterate.

As the reader will observe, and in order to keep this book proportional to its main objective, many of the simpler words and expressions have been deliberately excluded; readers, I'm sure, will be only too well acquainted with these, however, it does not preclude the reader from advising the writer/compiler of their existence.

The blank note pages, at the end, are left for your own use, and I would be pleased to hear from anyone, with an interest in the discovery of the lore and language of our great maritime history, who might add to, or enlighten me on the subject.

John Parker

WIND

Figure 01: Taken-aback

A1. (To be in first-class condition, or order)

This is an old classification given by Lloyd's Register of Shipping, indicating a ship's state of repair, and/or its sea worthiness. The 'A' is to recognize the 1st class standard of the vessel itself, and the '1' is for the good standard of the stowage, of her designated cargo.

When loose equipment, such as *ropes, anchors,* and *cables,* as well as the general construction and appearance of the vessel itself, met with Lloyd's criteria, the specification of *First Class* would be given. The highest classification for a ship and her cargo is 'A1'

Aback. (Taken-aback, surprised or shocked)

In maritime terms, it would describe a sailing ship trying to sail into a head wind, when the sails may well be pressed back against the masts and spars, therefore restricting further, forward movement. Under such circumstances, depending on the strength of the head wind, it was quite possible for the ship to be also driven backwards! (See also *Taken-aback,* and *Tack*)   (See Figure 01)

Abase or Debase. (To deride, humiliate, or to lower quality)

A very old, nautical expression, that means to pull up or to lower a ship's colours or flag. In other words, to degrade or bring someone or something down to a lower level.

Above board. (Legal and open to examination, seen to be of good business practice)
In nautical terms, it refers to everything on or above the deck of a sailing ship, hiding nothing from general view or scrutiny.

Abreast. (To be aware of all current and relevant conditions and circumstances)
This term was used when two ships were lying side by side, or alongside one another. Colloquially, it means to stay well informed of current matters, to keep up with your colleagues, and to be equal in the knowledge and awareness of what is happening around you.

Abroad. (Usually, to travel overseas)
An old word for *Spread*, describing the situation when all sails would be *Open* or *Spread out*. It also means to be away from one's home or homeport, or even *At large*.
The word suggests seafaring, but it could equally mean travelling away from familiar surroundings.

Adamant. (Resolute, resistant to persuasion)
A name that mariners, of a bygone age, gave to a mineral called *Magnetic oxide of iron*. It was the Chinese who first discovered this material, millennia ago, when they managed to adapt, and to attach it to a suspended iron bar. They even floated it in water, pasted to a piece of wood, when it would always point to the magnetic north. They considered it to be magi

cal, calling it *Guiding stone*. This material was then adapted for use in the manufacture of compasses. In the early days it was actually called *'Magic stone'*.

This mineral was also known as *Lodestone* or *Loadstone* and *Way stone*. Lodestone was almost exclusively used in the diamond industry. Possibly, this is the main reason why the word *Adamant* is used to mean *Positive*, and again because of its hardness in the way it would cut diamonds.

The *'North Star'* was also referred to as the *Lodestar*. In the middle ages, if a ship was to get lost in the fog, for instance, and the *Lodes man* or navigator was found to be at fault, it was not unheard of for him to be tied to the windlass, or some other suitable place on board ship, and to be beheaded, for the danger they believed he had created for his shipmates! (It is possible that the word Lode, in the word Lodestone, was translated for use in other types of mining of valuable minerals. i.e. Gold, Silver, Tin, etc. and not just Diamonds)

Adams Ale. (Drinking water)

Sailor's slang-name for fresh water, probably taken from the world's first man, Adam, and therefore taken to mean clear and pure water, that one would expect from the *Garden of Eden*. On long sea voyages, or when fresh water became scarce or rationed, it was almost certain that the limited supply, of fresh drinking water, would run out or turn foul and become undrinkable, so that any alcoholic drink would have been preferable. Therefore, pure fresh drinking water became known as *Adams Ale*. (See also *Addled*)

Addled. (Confused. Or gone off, as in addled egg)
A sailor's name for water that has *gone off*, or gone stale in the cask, and become virtually undrinkable, which was always possible on long sea voyages, between ports of call, before the supply of good, clean drinking-water could be replenished. The word *Addled* is taken from the old English expression *Adela*, meaning *liquid filth*. Colloquially, it can also mean to be muddled, or confused in the head, or 'Not all there' (*See also Adams Ale*)

Adrift. (To be floating free)
To lose one's moorings, to be at the mercy of the elements. A ship that is out of control. Colloquially, to be wide of the mark with all connections severed.

Advance. (To be given prepayment for an existing or future commitment)
On signing the ship's register, seamen would be paid an '*advance*' against future wages, enabling them to purchase personal requirements, such as special clothing or toiletries, which would not be available from the Purser, while the ship was at sea. The '*Advance*' usually amounted to one month's pay. Once received, some sailors would squander it on booze, women, and gambling, which meant that there would be very little, if any, left over for his other needs. (See '*Flogging a dead horse*').

Airy-Fairy (To be off-hand, to have a Devil may care attitude)
A fairly modern expression, and a derogatory term for a person serving in the Fleet Air Arm. Usually relating to the aircrew. 'Airey', meaning breeze, or to be in a draught. 'Fairy', meaning to fly, or to flit about as if on wings.

Aloof. (Acting superior, distant, unsympathetic)
A nautical expression that means to keep the ship's head or bows as close to the wind as possible, or windward, currently referred to as *The Luff*. It can also mean *A-Loft*, from the old English word *Lof*. And to get away from others by climbing *A-Loft*. Colloquially, it means to keep one's distance, or to stand apart from someone or something.

Any port in a storm. (Having to take whatever one can get, in times of trouble)
When sudden storms strike, a ship would be forced to find shelter, or take refuge, in the first available port or harbour, so at these times, any port would meet the needs.

Apparel (Clothing)
Equipment and fittings on board ship i.e. rigging, awnings, anchors, and small boats. (See also *'Awning'*)

At a loose end. (Wondering around, with nothing to do)

On occasions when crew members had very little work to do, the captain, or a senior officer, would expect the men to examine all ropes and rigging, to ensure that there was no damage from frayed, or loose ends. Faulty or stressed ropes would need to be bound or whipped to prevent further unravelling, or if all else failed, ropes and cables would have to be replaced. In heavy weather and storms, frayed or loose ropes, could be a potential danger to the ship's company, or even to the ship itself. (See also *'Fag end'*)

Awning. (A canvas shelter)

The word was first used in the early 1600s and is certainly of maritime origin: meaning a covering of cloth, probably over a window.

Back off. (To walk away from, leave alone, not interfere)

Originally, a whaling expression. Once a harpoon had struck its mark, the *Harpooners* would call out, *"Back off all"*, signifying a potential danger, especially if the whale gave a flurry with its tail, and then dived, taking the *Whaling Cutter* and her crew down with it, possibly drowning some, if not all, of the seven-man crew.

Bail. (Surety for the temporary release of a suspected criminal)

This derives from the French 'Baillier' - to deliver on trust, and usage dates back to the 14th century.

Nautically, it means to *move overboard*. This was cargo illegally obtained, and held by the authorities. This cargo was not allowed to be removed or taken on bail, until legal permission had been obtained, and mutual arrangements made for its removal. It is also a term used for a signal or beacon giving a light, signifying that permission is given for a vessel to leave port.

Baling or bailing out. (To release from difficulty, come to the rescue of someone)
Nautically, it is the ladling of water out of a boat. The word derives from 'Baile', which is an early name for a bucket, and not, as one might imagine, a cross between a bucket and a pail. Usage has been known since the 17th century.

Bang on. (Right, correct, perfect timing.)
Sailor's slang for *'right on target'*, referring to the targeting of their guns. In this day and age it means *'Correct'* or *'Right on time'*, sometimes used as meaning: talking too much.

Barge. (To bump into, or to collide with someone, or something)
This is a flat-bottomed, small vessel (*A Flatner for instance*) used for ferrying goods, via rivers, when mud banks could present a problem. It also describes the ability to push in, or barge into narrow places between smaller vessels, and to gain access to other boats or to dry land.

Bargepole. (Not to be touched with a 'Bargepole')
A Bargepole is a long, heavy implement, used aboard barges to fend off other craft or obstacles. Usually, it would be tipped with a metal spike or hook. If it were possible to manoeuvre a barge between larger craft, without touching it, then the 'Bargee' would not be 'touching it with a bargepole'. Colloquially the expression would mean to avoid something, or someone, you mistrust or dislike.

Batten down the hatches. (To prepare, or protect oneself, and/or others, or things, from ensuing problems)
In nautical terms, a 'batten' refers to a strip of wood or metal, for securing a tarpaulin (some times as extra protection) over the ship's hatchways. A hatchway is an opening, on a ship's deck, used for lowering cargo into the hold. Protecting this cargo, in stormy weather, would be most essential, so when the order came to: 'Batten down the hatches,' it meant exactly that: to cover hatches, with tarpaulin, and make secure with 'battens'. Colloquially, it is a phrase meaning, to prepare oneself for an eventual problem.

Beaker. (A drinking vessel)
A wooden water-keg found on small ships or boats shore-side. Colloquially, it is a mug, glass, or a drinking vessel. (See also *'Fill your boots'*)

Beam-ends. (To be out of luck, or in serious financial trouble.)

Describes a ship, lying completely on her side, with the ship's beams vertical rather than horizontal. A dangerous situation to be in, with little hope of getting back into an upright position, especially for a large vessel. *Beams* being a ship's ribs, or beam supports, fitted across the width of the hull. (See Figure 02.)

Bearings. (To establish the heading and direction one needs to be taking.)

A maritime expression which means to establish position and direction, or to find a position of advantage, or 'bear down' on, or 'lie off', or 'bear off' in a certain direction.

Figure 02: Beam-ends

Bearing up. (Keeping one's spirits up. Doing the best one can in difficult circumstances)
A ship's heading, relative to the wind. When a ship *'Bears away'*, it means that she is steering further away from the wind. To *'Bear down'* means that she is heading towards her target or destination. *'Bearing up'* suggests making the best of a prevailing wind or situation.

Beat. (To beat about the bush, for instance, or to win)
Nautically, to move or to Tack or Zigzag one-way then another, against erratic changes in wind and weather. Sailing to windward is known as *'Beating to windward'*. Colloquially, it means to fuss around, do something in an indirect fashion.

Bender. (Going out with the sole purpose of getting drunk.)
A *Bender* is a piece of equipment used to bend small crossbows. (At one time used for the coiling of ropes.) *'Strike out for a bend'* is a term applied to rope coiling. The word is of nautical origin and could reflect a seaman's slang to get drunk, or to get *'Tight'*. A bend is a shipboard knot, which is tied very tight.

Bend over backwards. (Doing everything possible to help)
This is certainly a boating or maritime expression. When pulling on the oars, it would be necessary, at times, to lean or bend over backwards using great effort, in order to get good leverage on the oars. A *bend* is also a turn, or a knot in a rope. (*See also Bender*)

Between the devil and the deep blue sea. (A decision that could mean trouble either way)

Pity the poor sailor working to repair a leaking plank, over the side of his ship, when she was tossing and pitching about in rough weather, and being battered by strong winds. The most awkward, the longest plank outboard of a wooden ship, or the deck seam immediately adjacent to the vessel's side, is called *The devil*, so the poor sailor doing these repairs, outboard of the ship, would literally be between *the devil and the deep blue sea*. One slip and he would disappear, probably unnoticed, and be gone without trace. (*See also Devil to pay*)

Bib. (Protection of sorts)

A bracket situated under the *trestletree* of a ship at the base of a mast, which resembles a child's bib, the mast representing a child's neck. This is used mostly on larger sailing vessels. On smaller craft, the mast would more than likely be supported by *The Stays*, or go through the deck and be secured in the Ship's Hold.

Bible. (The Holy Bible)

A small block of *Sandstone* or *Pumice* used for scouring the ship's deck: so named because mariners would have to kneel to do the job of scrubbing, which made them look as though they were praying. The sandstone, used in this way, was also named *Holystone* (this would be *pumice* or *lava stone*).

Bilge. (A load of nonsense, or rubbish)
This is a nautical expression, meaning a swollen bag, or leather bottle; the shape being very similar to that of a ship's hull. (*See also Fill your boots.*) A Bilge means a protuberance, a hump, or a curved barrel, full of waste.

Bitter end. (To stick it out to the very end)
On sailing ships, anchors were fixed, with ropes or cables, to bollards which were usually made from iron but were sometimes made from heavy timbers called *Bitts* or *fore bitts*; when anchors were not held at the *Cathead*, (two short beams, projecting horizontally, either side of the bows.) and when anchors were lowered to the maximum depth that rope or cable would allow. The part left aboard, above the water, was called '*The bitter end*'. Sailors, when allowed to do so, could sit on these 'Bitts', between tasks, to take a rest. Songs sung during these periods of rest were called *Forbitters*, as opposed to other working songs that are called *Shanties*. (See '*Shanty*')   (See Figure 03)

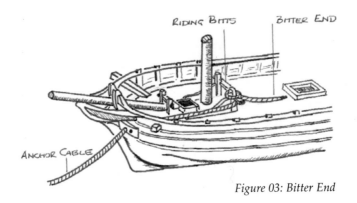

Figure 03: Bitter End

Blazer. (Smart casual-Jacket, or part of an officer's uniform)

In the 1850s, it became the custom for captains and ship's masters to purchase uniforms for the crew. The ship's officers, however, were supplied with short, dark coats, as part of their uniform, to separate their appearance from the rest of the crew. The most memorable was the crew of HMS *Blazer*, reputedly the first ship to accept this form of dress, and was where the name Blazer originated.

Blind eye. (To choose not to see)

Reputedly, from the days of Admiral Lord Nelson, who was supposedly blinded in one eye. That he was completely blinded in either of his eyes is unsubstantiated, although his sight was impaired, for a period of time, following an injury at the battle of Copenhagen in 1801, when a musket ball seared across his forehead and the side of his cheek. Commander Admiral Parker ordered Nelson to withdraw from this battle position, but Nelson held his telescope to his, then, partially blinded eye, and was said to be unable to read the signal! As we would say he *'looked the other way'* or *'turned a blind eye'*.

Blood money. (Money earned with sweat and hard graft)

The admiralty paid a bounty for the capture, or apprehension, of smugglers. A cash reward was also paid to Innkeepers, Pressgangs, and owners of Boarding houses, when they informed the navy of drunks, and other individuals, seemingly fit and capable of serving aboard Royal Navy Ships.

Bluff. (To deceive someone into believing other than the truth)

Bluff refers to the large, and wide part of the bows of a ship, and to warships in particular. Seemingly, to exaggerate the true size when being approached head on by enemy ships. The perceived size of *The Bluff* would leave the enemy in some doubt as to the true size and capabilities of the approaching vessel, and hopefully scare it off. On the negative side, it could do the opposite, and the ship would then become an easy target for the enemy from this angle.

Board. (A long table, or room, where senior officers would meet)

The Board refers to the outside of a ship. To go '*By the Board*' would either mean a person falling overboard, or a piece of the ship's superstructure, such as a mast or spar, falling overboard. The word A-Board would mean to retrieve that which has fallen overboard. Colloquially, 'to go by the board' would mean to be neglected, omitted, passed over, or discarded.

Bolster. (To boost confidence)

A 'Bolster' would have been used on older sailing ships. It is a piece of hard or soft wood, used to prevent chafing when sails or ropes might rub against the ship's superstructure. Bolsters are also used for lining the 'Hawseholes' (through which anchor cables run) to prevent the anchor cables rubbing against the 'Hawsehole cheeks'. Bolsters would sometimes be covered with canvas to prevent wear and tear to the more sensitive parts of a ship. As a point of interest, the wrinkled stocking-type materials, used around a ship's moving rigging, to prevent the chafing of sails, are called 'Baggy wrinkles'. 'Bolster' is also a term used for a hard, padded pillow, or as an item of bedding, such as a head or back support.

Bombshell. (An unexpected and shocking event)
A mortar-firing canon usually placed adjacent to the foredeck, where it would be easier to manoeuvre into position, for the shelling of places ashore. A Bombshell, in maritime terms, is usually a fused bomb that is timed to explode on landing; in these cases, they would either be dropped from a height or propelled by a mortar, and on landing, would be totally unexpected.

Bonnet. (Protective headwear)
An additional piece of canvas sailcloth, attached to the foot of 'jibs', or the 'fore and aft' sails, in order to attract the wind, so helping the forward movement of the ship. The unbuttoned bonnet is for storm purposes and would give unlimited protection; hence the word Bonnet is used for a covering protecting the head.

Booby. (A large breasted seabird of the gannet family)
Used by sailors as a slang word for boobs or breasts, also a slang word for a stupid mistake or an error of

judgement, possibly because the Booby-bird was so easily caught.

Boot up. (Common word these days for starting-up a computer)
In days of sail, especially on warships, crew-members would have little time to go to a central water supply to slake their thirst. Most would have a leather bottle, tied to their belts, to hold drinking water: this was called '*a boot*'. When time permitted, they would be allowed to replenish their Boots with water, hence the expression, 'Fill your boots.'

Bowing and Scraping. (Showing one's inferior position, being servile.)
An officer's cocked hat was nicknamed 'A Scraper'. To Bow and Scrape originally meant doffing one's hat, as a mark of respect, or servility; bowing, as well, was a form of salute to a superior officer. Without headwear, the touching of one's forelock would be a customary form of salute, or subservience. Colloquially, it is taken as fawning around someone superior.

Brace of shakes. (A short time, i.e. a couple of minutes.)
A measurement of time, based on the shimmering or shaking of sails, coming into the wind, which would usually be a very sudden happening. This figure of speech also means a short-timed interval, such as: '*Back in a minute*', or as the saying goes: '*Back in a brace of shakes*', or: '*Back in a couple of shakes*'.

Brace up! (To prepare oneself for difficulties, or a shock, or to get a grip.)
The Brace is a rope or chain that controls horizontal/sideways movement of a Yard, from which a square sail hangs. It could also be the means by which a sail is set, in order to catch the wind. A Brace can also be a heavy cable, supporting a mast, so that it's braced and ready for the wind.

Brass Monkey. (Very cold)
This term was used as far back as the 1700s. A Brass Monkey is a tray, made of brass, which was placed close to the canons on a ship's gun-deck, in order to hold the canon-balls, prior to loading them into the muzzle. In battle, it was quite possible for ice-cold sea-water to be showered on board, and to wash over these brass trays, which would make the canon balls freeze together. Also note Powder Monkey, though not a term used in everyday language, it was a title given to young boys who were employed to carry gun powder, from the ship's powder magazine, in order to load up the 'Monkeys' with fresh ammunition. (See Figure 04)

Breach. (To break through something, with force)
A term used when sea breaks across the deck of a ship. It is also a forced opening in a wall or fortification, caused by canon or gunfire explosives, or a Bombshell. (See Bombshell)

Figure 04: Brass Monkey

Bristol fashion. (Neat, clean and tidy)
A saying based on the good reputation of the ships that sailed out of Bristol: i.e. all vessels leaving this port were reputed to be in good and proper order. This was so, until the port of Liverpool came into being, and competition became fierce. From then, the orderly fashion, which was Bristol's pride and joy, started to slip. (See also Shipshape and Bristol fashion)

Broach. (To raise a matter for discussion)
A term used when a vessel has been driven too hard, and consequently slewed sideways. In some cases, sails are caught: Flat a back, making it possible for masts to break. Also means to break into a barrel, or to open a bottle.

Broad in the beam. (A large and shapely woman, viewed from behind)
The width of a ship from port to starboard, usually looking at it from the stern or back end of a ship.

Bully. (A person who uses strength or power to coerce others weaker than themselves)
In naval terms, 'Bully' would mean strong and powerful, good and well respected. A 'Bully crew' would be a friendly hardworking bunch of men. A Bully, these days, could still warrant one or two of these descriptions, but is now regarded mainly as someone who uses strength and power to cause fear, and to override a weaker person.

Bumper. (A protective buffer)
Nautically, the term used for large logs or pieces of timber, dangled over the ship's side, to protect her from icy conditions should the sea freeze over. At sea level, it was thought that a 'bumper' would help to stop the ship from being crushed, when in pack ice; they were also used to stop damage to the ship's hull, when it was tied up in dock. Bumper also refers to a large measure of beer or spirits.

Burning one's boats. (To leave everything behind, to commit oneself irrevocably.)
In ancient times, when a ship was in danger of capture, rather than allowing the boat or ship to be seized, it was often considered a better option to destroy them by fire, in order to avoid handing them over to the enemy.

Buttock, or 'b-tak' in Greek. (Lower rear-part of the human body)
The width and breadth of a ship's stern, which has the *'Counter'* above it, the *'bilge'* below, the *'stern post'* in the middle, and the *'quarter'* at her side. A ship could be said to have broad or narrow buttocks, depending on the width of her Stern or Counter.

Button. (On the button - spot on, or exactly right)
The button is situated on the tops of masts, or the highest point of a ship above the water line. In the old days of sail, the most agile crew member would probably climb to the top, usually using rigging and shrouds, (See shrouds) in order to balance on the Button or The Truck. This often happened when the ship was on show or display, or when entering port. Colloquially, *'on the button'* would mean: 'to be spot on', or 'absolutely correct.' (See 'Skyscraper')

Bye and bye. (Or by and by)
To sail a vessel 'By the wind', or to sail her as close to the wind as possible, with all her sails hard in and her bows pointing towards the wind, would be making slow progress. In other words, waiting for a certain time - as in 'By and by'. (Originally Bi-bi was meant as, side-by-side.) The second 'By', 'Bi', or 'Bye', was used to emphasize the difficulties experienced by having to sail this way. Colloquially, 'By and By' means, in a little while.

By and large. (In general, all things taken into account)
When a vessel is sailing into the wind, she is said to be sailing *'By and large'*, or near to the wind, but not fully on to it; so that the leading edge of each sail is still setting as close to the wind as possible. To sail slightly off wind, makes it easier for the helmsman to steer. (Give or take a little)

Carry the can. (To take the blame)
Colloquially, it means to accept overall responsibility for a blunder. Nautically, it refers to the responsibility of junior ranks to remove any waste, or to fetch and carry for their superiors.

Catch a packet. (Costing a lot of money)
Probably relates to 'Packet-ships' delivering and collecting mail, or cargo, to and from ships in port. Speed was always of the essence, so sailors were hard pushed to keep up. This was an expensive way of collecting and delivering; missing a ship could cost them dearly, so, in other words, they would be 'Catching a packet.' (See 'Packet')

Catwalk. (Gangway / Stage)
A narrow passageway between fore (The Cathead) and aft (The Poop-deck), situated just inside the outermost edge of a ship, connecting the poop deck to the forecastle (fo'c'sle). It can also mean a gangway without any form of handrail or hand rope. A dangerous place to be in heavy weather, without a safety line, but necessary

for deck-crews to perform daily tasks, without getting in the way of other deck-workers. Colloquially, it is a narrow platform where fashion-models walk.

Chantey. (See Shanty)
From the French: to Chanter or to Chunter on.

Chewing the fat. (Talking things over or just having a chat)
Popular 19th century saying, among seamen. In those days, salted fatty-beef was part of a seaman's daily diet. Prolonged chewing would soften the meat and make consumption of it a little more bearable.

Chock-a-block. (Crowded or crammed full)
Describes the position of two pulley blocks that come together when hauling or pulling ropes, and where no further movement is possible. The Choc is a kind of wedge, and the Block is the body of the actual pulley. (See Figure 05)

Chop-chop! (An order to, 'Hurry up', or 'Make it snappy')
A saying that originated in the 1700s, from the Cantonese language, in the South China seas, from the words, 'K'wai-k'wai', meaning: 'to hurry up', and, reputedly, adapted by British sailors. (There is suggestion, that a similar phrase was used some 200 years prior to this.) Apart from the meaning in both languages, it is not known how this expression relates, one to the other, as far as the pronunciation is concerned.

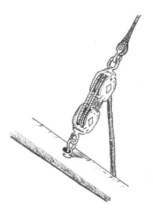

Figure 05:
Choc-a-block

Clean bill of health. (Notification of being fit and healthy)
Ships, arriving at a port-of-call, would need to be checked and cleared by local authorities, to ensure that no communicable diseases were present, on board, amongst the cargoes or ships crews. Once cleared, they would be given a clean bill of health.

Clean Slate. (A fresh start)
In the early days of sail, the course steered by a ship was recorded, initially, onto a slate, and then into the Deck-log. At the start of each watch, the Watch Commander, after noting the previous course taken and making the necessary corrections, would wipe the slate clean. Each new Watch Commander would follow this same procedure. In other words, past and previous occurrences would be wiped off, after being recorded in the Deck-log, and a new and clean slate started.

Clean sweep. (To wipe out past imputations/ misdemeanours)

This expression originally came from the Dutch navy, when it was a force to be reckoned with. Each ship would hoist a broom to their masthead, to show that they were capable of sweeping the seas free of their enemies. Some would say it means that the sea has washed across the deck, removing much loose equipment and debris.

Clear as a bell. (Excellent hearing, or acute perception.)

At sea, when all is calm and still, with maybe some mist or fog around, sound would travel further and be clearer than usual. So, whenever the ship's bell sounded, it was likely to be heard by other vessels in the vicinity, and more importantly, by all crewmembers. Colloquially, as well as referring to good hearing, it is taken as meaning to have a good understanding of things or matters.

Clear the decks. (Get everything out of the way.)

Certainly on warships, before battle commenced, speed was important. Usually the order to prepare for action would come via a drumbeat (Beating to quarters). This would instruct the crew to clear away loose and unnecessary items, on decks, that were likely to impede progress.

Clewed up. (Very knowledgeable, particularly at work)

A 'Clew' is the aftermost bottom corner of a square sail, or a 'fore and aft' sail, and is located at the sail's bottom corners, to which the 'Clew lines' are attached. (See also Sheets.) These are the means by which sails are hoisted up to the yards or to the masts. (The first step towards furling sails or to be clued up) (See Figure 06)

Close to the wind. (Taking a chance)

To sail as near to the wind, and as far as possible into the wind, whilst 'making way', or 'headway'. In other words, it means operating in a risky fashion, in order to navigate the ship onto a set course. Sailing close to the wind is always a chancy business.

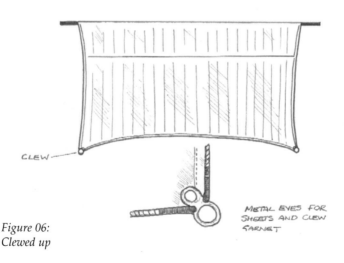

CLEW

METAL EYES FOR SHEETS AND CLEW GARNET

Figure 06:
Clewed up

Coast is clear. (All is well to continue)
Comes from the old days of smuggling and wrecking, when gang members posted lookouts to avoid the Excise men. This practice was widely used in the West Country - it being close to the French coast, and where currents and tides are at their most dangerous. Wreckers would show lights, from headlands, which would sometimes be tied to donkeys or horses, to imitate a ship bobbing at anchor in the harbour. This would lure unsuspecting merchantmen onto the reefs and rocks, fooling them into believing that 'The coast was clear.'

Cocked hat. (Knock into a cocked hat - to be utterly defeated)
This was a form of headdress worn by officers. Because of its shape, it would sometimes be used to *triangulate* the ship's position. This was not a very precise method of navigating, but was permissible in olden times, when navigation was far from accurate, and readings from old charts and equipment could be wrong. Nowadays, the term is taken to mean totally defeated.

Cock-up. (A big mistake)
The source of this expression is *Cockbill* or *a-cockbill*, referring to the state of the anchor when hoisted up and hung onto the *Cathead*. The *bill* is the pointed end of the *fluke* of the anchor. (The part that digs into the seabed) It is possible for an anchor to become twisted, in strong winds, (if not secured) when *bills* are 'cocked up', i.e. both pointing skyward. If the anchor should be

dropped while in the wrong position, it could cause great damage to the side of the ship: this would be a disaster, a so-called 'Cock-up.'(*See also Fluke*) Some say it refers to the hammer of a musket when pulled back too far and cocking the weapon, as this could cause the spring to break, and render the firearm temporarily uséless.

Collar. (Neck-wear)
A maritime word for an 'Eye splic', or the metal ring around the wreath, at the end of a shroud (or stay), that goes over a masthead. (See Shroud) Also a term used for the unthreaded neck of a bolt.

Copper-bottomed. (An absolute guarantee)
Sheathing of a ship's hull, with copper plate, helped to preserve timbers from rotting, or attracting barnacles and other sea borne termites, including weed and the infestation of worm. The copper plating could also have the effect of making the vessel smoother, below the water-line, thus helping to make her faster when under sail. This practice officially began in 1761.

Corker. (Someone or something exceptionally good, beautiful or worthwhile)
The word *Corker* was, more than likely, taken from the maritime word *Caulker*. This is the name of a person who works at making the ship's seams waterproof. When at sea, this could be a most hazardous job. Calling a sailor, by using this title, would be seen as a compliment. (*See also: Between the devil and the deep blue*

sea) It might also be *Cawker*, which was to take a glass of spirits, especially in the morning.

Couple of shakes. (A short period of time)
(*See: Brace of shakes.*)

Crack on (To move on quickly)
Nautically, it means to set sail and to proceed as quickly as possible, within safety limits. This term, 'Crack on regardless' was used on the old mail-ships, when safety was more or less sacrificed for the extra speed, and penalties would be incurred for late delivery.

Craft. (A skill or trade)
In days gone by, it referred to the skill needed for making and sailing boats or ships, which was then called 'A Craft'. These days, it would cover almost all acquired skills.

Crimp (A Hairdressing term, or the crimping or cramping of one's style)
To hinder or obstruct. A Crimp was a person who, single handedly, would kidnap seamen, and, for payment, would deliver them to a vessel that was short-handed.

Crossing the line. (Overstepping the mark)
It is traditional for passengers and crew, aboard ship, (especially Royal Navy ships) to undergo the ceremony of Crossing the line. Senior crew-members would dress up as King Neptune, Queen Amphritite and Davy Jones, to assist seamen and passengers in the

celebration of Crossing the line (the equator) for the first time. These victims would be called *'Pollywags'*. Following a successful ceremony, they would be entitled to use the name Shellback. These days the victims would normally be washed and shaved in seawater, and given a certificate as proof of their crossing the line. But in years gone by, this ceremony often consisted of various forms of torture, brutality, and degradation. Eventually the victim might be thrown overboard, sometimes with loss of life! This would of course be Overstepping the mark or Crossing the line.

Cut and run. (Break loose and escape as fast as possible)
This phrase originates from the year 1704. Older battleships would, more than likely, have anchor cables made from hemp. If taken by surprise by an enemy ship, rather than waste valuable time making good their escape, the order would be given to cut the anchor cable, the preference being to lose the anchor rather than being captured. It could also mean the process of furling sails, onto the yards, using light ropes; these could easily be cut, enabling the sails to fall quickly, helping them to fill with wind for a fast getaway. (See also Give someone the slip)

Cut of his jib. (An outward appearance, or style)
The cut or condition of a ship's Jib or foresail signified the general quality of the complete vessel, which could be good or bad.

Dab hand. (A person skilled at a particular job)
A '*Dab hand*', at one time, referred to a sailor whose duties included painting or the dabbing on of paint, he would also be expected to perform other odd, unskilled jobs aboard ship. After much experience, he would be considered suitably adept at these allotted tasks, and would be classed as a Dab hand at several more tasks.

Dead in the water. (A good plan or idea that does not come to fruition)
This is a nautical expression from the great days of sail. When there was no wind to drive the ship, it would lie motionless and useless, and so termed: Dead in the water.

Dead on time. (Arrival-time being exactly right)
Said to derive from sea lore, in the old belief: 'when one's time had come to move on to the next life, then death would surely come about at that allotted, and precise time.' Or in other words, it would be, dead on time. ('Fiddlers Green', is a place between heaven and hell, where all dead sailors are supposed to go) or *Kismet*, meaning to meet one's fate.

Dead reckoning. (An accurate measurement)
Originally called 'Decided reckoning,' later shortened to De'd reckoning, in much the same way one would abbreviate the word received to rec'd. When the weather was relatively calm, it was possible to take accurate readings from the earth's curvature, or the

stars. (See also Plane sailing.) Taking readings in adverse weather conditions would be difficult and often inaccurate, so navigation, even over short distances in such conditions, would become almost impossible. (See also 'Scraper')

Dead wood. (Material, or people, discarded after use)
Comes from the shipbuilding trade. This was the job of laying wooden blocks in a keel, under construction, in order to keep the balance of the ship whilst it was being built. These blocks were not essential to the ship itself, and were of no other practical use, other than to keep the keel rigid in order to make construction work a great deal easier; after which they would be discarded, so termed as dead wood.

Derrick. (Heavy lifting device, found in docks or on building sites)
Named after the public hangman, Mister Derrick of Tynham prison. Wooden lifting gear, used to load and unload cargo ships, that resembled Mister Derrick's invention of using a single spar, to hoist the condemned person into the air, rather than the customary use of a hangman's rope over a scaffold spar.

Deserting a sinking ship. (To walk away from a disastrous situation)
Usually referred to as: Rats deserting a sinking ship. It was said that rats always seemed to know when it was time to leave a ship, which was either when it was sinking, or when it was coming into harbour.

Devil to pay. (A threatened punishment.)
This is an ancient seafaring term meaning: a task very difficult to perform. It originates from the old 'Caulkers' language and the ships 'Garboard-seam' (longest external seam of a ship's hull) universally known as 'The devil' and difficult to work when caulking, or filling gaps with pitch or tar, or for sealing leaky gaps in the ship's timbers. A very dangerous and sometimes fatal place to be in stormy weather, hence the saying, 'Between the devil and the deep blue sea'. (See also 'Corker')

Dip out. (Avoid involvement.)
Origin unsure, but it was most certainly an expression used in the Navy. It may have something to do with the term 'Pusser's dip,' which was the old, reject oil and grease from the galley, which could be kept by the ship's Purser for resale when the vessel was in port or in dock, where it would probably be used to make up candles and lantern fuel.

Does not cut much ice. (Makes little or no impression.)
A wooden sailing-ship would make little, or no progress, if crew attempted to manoeuvre it through pack ice, doing so, would probably end up with the ship being crushed and rendered useless. (See 'Bolster')

Dogsbody. (A drudge, someone of lower status expected to be at everyone's beck and call)
Mainly attributed to passenger ships, where leftover food would be mixed with ships' biscuits, then reheated and served-up to the crew. Also a tasteless meal, referred to by the crew as a *'dog's body'*, which they were expected to eat and even to approve of. It is also nautical slang for a junior officer.

Doldrums. (Mentally and/or physically in a depressed state.)
When a ship lies becalmed, usually just north or south of the equator between the trade wind systems, the situation could sometimes last for weeks on end, leaving the ship and crew in a depressed state. The captain might then order the crew to launch boats, in an effort to tow the ship to where the wind was likely to be, and so move on. This operation had a dual effect on the crew i.e. they were kept busy and at the same time, doing something positive to get out of the doldrums. (See also 'Whistling up a wind')

Donkey's breakfast. (Scruffily dressed.)
This is a merchant seaman's name for his mattress or 'Pallyass', which was a large canvas bag filled with straw, likened to a donkey's breakfast. Such mattresses were usually restricted for use on wooden bunks, and not for hammocks, (which were usually stuffed with horsehair.)

Donkeywork. (Very heavy work.)
This historical phrase refers to a 'Donkey engine' that was used to crane the heaviest cargoes, such as bulk timber, into and out of a ship's hold, or onto the deck.

Dressing-down. (To be reprimanded)
This expression dates back to the mid 1600s. In maritime terms, it meant dressing the rigging with a preservative such as oil or tar. A horrible job, usually handed out to miscreants or unskilled crewmembers.

Earmarked. (An identifying mark, a person or thing set aside for a special purpose)
Used in old maritime language, also used universally in one guise or another. Miscreants, committing a crime in the navy, would have one of their ears pierced with a nail, to show everyone that the person concerned was a shipboard criminal. If both ears were pierced, that person would be considered to be a habitual offender. Sometimes the offender would wear an earring to try to cover his guilt. As far as is known, this was why sailors started wearing earrings.

Earring. (Jewellery designed for wearing solely on the ears)
In maritime language, a small piece of rope used to fasten the corners of a square sail, to the yardarm, by either threading it through an eyelet, or securing the rope around the tip of the spar.

Eat my hat. (An expression of surprise when admitting to being wrong)
Sailors would keep 'Plugs' (or Quids) of chewed tobacco inside the lining of their hats. The juices, from this chewed tobacco, would soak into the hat's lining. When there was no further supply of tobacco available, they would take out their hatbands and suck or chew on these instead!

Edge away. (To ease away from a threatening situation)
This was a gradual changing of a ship's course, in order to ease away from the wind.

Fag-end. (Cigarette end)
This is the last part, or remnant of frayed rope, or the end of a worn rope or lashing. (See also 'Fagged out') (Figure 07)

Fagged-out. (Worn out)
The 'Fag end' is generally referred to as a cigarette end. In naval terms, it would be the last possible bit of rope that could be of any use. It also refers to the un-whipped end of rope that has been in constant use. Poor quality, of the rope itself, would determine whether or not it should be discarded, or soaked in 'Dip' (see Dip-out) to make wicks for candles.

Figure 07:
Fag-end

Fair enough. (An acceptable situation)
A phrase commonly used at sea, meaning to 'shape' or adjust something until it fits a given situation. In seaman's terms, 'Fair' means favourable (the opposite of 'Foul') as in 'Fairway', or a clear, navigable passage for vessels entering or leaving port.

Fall foul. (To come into conflict with, or to quarrel)
Nautically, it could mean the foul smell of a ship's hold. Or an unsuitable anchorage, which allowed the vessel to swing on its moorings, or strike against another ship.

Fathom. (To think something through, comprehend a problem)
A 'Fathom' is approximately a six-foot depth of water, or 1.828 metres. (See also *'Swinging the lead'*) When

measuring the depth of draught (the distance below the water line, to the under side of the vessel, or the sea bed) in shallow muddy water, it could be difficult to be sure of the true depth, and was said to be "difficult to fathom". Fathom or Faethm is an Anglo-Saxon word meaning 'outstretched arms', which would have been a method used to estimate a length of 6 feet.

Feeling blue. (Sad and dispirited)
A custom dating back to the old sailing ships of centuries ago, especially when on long sea voyages. If the ship's captain was lost, or had died at sea, a senior officer would probably have flown a blue flag, and would, very possibly, have had a blue band painted around the ship's entire hull as a sign of respect when returning to the vessel's home port.

Fend off. (To keep away from, or to ward off an attack)
A nautical expression that means to push away from another vessel or obstacle. A shortened version of 'Fender'. Fenders are used to protect a ship's sides from damage. In common use, fenders would be planks of wood or heavy netting, and in latter years, old rubber tyres.

Fiddle. (A violin)
This nautical word 'Fiddle' probably comes from the names of a pair of blocks used for hauling ropes (See Figure 08). Put together, the larger block would be above the smaller one, and linked in this way, they

Figure 08:
Fiddle Blocks

would resemble a violin. They would also lie flatter to a mast or spar than a double block might do. The movement between the two blocks suggests the expression that one block would be 'fiddling' the other, thus helping to 'work a fiddle'. This expression is also associated with a sailing ship's wooden eating-plates, (used to avoid spillage on deck) which were also called fiddles. (See 'Square meal') Spillage of food would make decking slippery, so any movement on the ship's deck could become hazardous. When spillage happened, the person causing it might be said to be 'On the fiddle'.

Field day. (An exciting or busy time)
Not specifically a maritime saying, although it does have naval connotations. Basically, it means to apply a bit of 'Spit and polish,' both above and below decks, in preparation for a ship's inspection. It would include

touching up paintwork, *(See 'Dab-Hand')* scrubbing decks, polishing brass, etc. Colloquially, it would mean to work hard, or to hold an enjoyable event.

Figurehead. (A respected leader of an organization)
The figurehead, on any vessel, would usually be situated at the foremost part of a ship's hull or bow; all on board would treat it with great respect and reverence, embodying the soul of the ship itself, just as they would the ship's colours. Years ago, it would have been unthinkable to go to sea without a figurehead - it was considered dangerous or at best risky, by a superstitious crew. The figureheads on ships of yesteryear were usually female, (although, unusually, some heroes, such as Admiral Nelson, might be in evidence.) Going back even further, vessels would have been dedicated to goddesses, by the Romans and Greeks, and is therefore one of the many reasons why ships are referred to as 'She' or 'Her'. (See Figure 09)

Figure 09:
Figure head

Fill your boots. (See 'Boot up')

First-rate. (High-class, or excellent.)
Originally a Royal Navy classing for the largest and best ships of the line, such as 'HMS *Victory*'. This expression started life in about 1670, for ships with 100 or more guns, and carrying a crew of 800 or more men, also for ships having a dispersal weight of 2000, or more, tons. Because of their size, these ships could be slow and ponderous of movement; even so, they would still be classed as 'first rate ships'.

Flake out. (To drop from Exhaustion.)
The operation of laying out the anchor cable, ready for inspection, and for the repair or replacement of the same. Weak or damaged chain links, or cordage, would be replaced or repaired as necessary. Once inspected, and found to be in good order, the cable would be classified and rewound, or 'Flaked down clear,' over the side of the ship, ready for use. It also refers to a cradle used for lowering down the side of a ship, in order to carry out repairs, or for re-caulking procedures. The laying down of the anchor cable, would also relate to a person, lying down for a rest, being said to be, 'Flaked out.'

Flash in the pan. (A promising start that turns to failure)
An expressive metaphor for a musket, or canon, that misfires. If the atmosphere were excessively moist, causing the wad of gunpowder (loaded into the muz-

zle) to become damp, then the act of firing the shot, or ball, would ignite the drier gunpowder (which would have been loaded into the ignition pan). This would leave the canon or musket still loaded-up, but unfired and temporarily useless. So leaving a 'flash in the pan', all to no avail.

Flogging a dead horse. (Energy wasted by hard work, all to no avail.)

A seaman would normally receive one month's payment for *'signing on'* before a voyage; this payment was called an *'Advance'*, which was meant to be used for personal equipment and clothing for the voyage. This *'advance'* though, was usually spent on wine, women, and gambling. The *'Dead horse'*, referred to, was the sailor himself who had to work like a donkey (or a horse) for a month, without any further payment, and as far as the sailor was concerned, he believed himself to be working for nothing. (*See also Advance*)

Fluke. (More by luck than judgement)

A 'Fluke' is part of the anchor that catches a rock or a protrusion; capable and strong enough to stop a ship from drifting (*See Figure 10*). Once the anchor has been dropped it might not be possible to see the seabed, so it would be considered to be more luck than judgement, or a *'Fluke'*, to find that the anchor had been successfully secured, in spite of working blind to do so. *'Fluke,' Flook,' 'Fluke,'* or *'Fluck'*, are also the names of flat fish or flounders. There are similarities between the shape of the 'Fluke' of an anchor and a flat fish - see also 'cock-up .

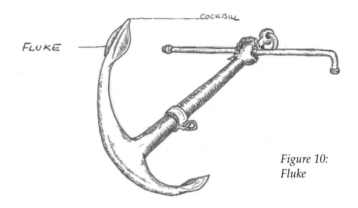

Figure 10:
Fluke

Fly-by-night. (An irresponsible and unreliable person)
The name was originally given to an extra sail, or a 'Fly sail', used to increase the sailing speed. This was usually a square sail set on a temporary yard when the wind came directly from astern. It could be erected and taken down quickly and was often used on fast clipper-ships, to increase speed, especially when in competition with others. If the wind were favourable, the 'Fly-sail' would sometimes be used at night, under cover of darkness. Hence the expression: 'Fly-by-night'. (See also Flyer.)

Flyer. (An ambitious, or outstanding person, or to take a chance)
'Flyer' is the name given to a fast clipper ship or a fast sailing vessel, usually a Tea Clipper.

Flying colours. (Successful in the extreme.)
In the early 1700s, the English navy flew their flags (or colours) when sailing into port, and if possible in line

with the river or dock-side, in order to be in full view of lookers-on; hence the saying: 'Passed with flying colours'. It was also a sign of victory. Hoisting their colours as high as possible up the masts, along with other ships in a victory parade, stood to demonstrate their successes in battle.

Frisbee. (A saucer shaped dish used as a cooking utensil. A round, plastic play dish)
In the modern navy, a '*Frisbee*' is a flat, dish-shaped, cooking utensil, made either of aluminium or stainless steel, which would be spun, playfully, over the cooking pots, in order to save walking-time, in the galley. It is also a plastic play-dish for spinning one to another. It is unsure which description came first, the naval cooking implement or the play-dish.

Full-flood. (Non-stop talking, or outburst of tears.)
A maritime phrase used to describe fast-flowing water on the ebb or flood tides. It also describes a person giving, for instance, a detailed and lengthy oratory.

Gaff. (To 'Blow the gaff' is to reveal a plot or secret)
Aboard ship, the 'Gaff' is a spar used to extend the fore and aft sails that are not set on the Stays. The fore-end of the 'Gaff' is called 'The Jaw,' which is secured by a 'Jaw rope'; if this should be blown out of position by a strong wind, it would be said to have 'Blown the Gaff'. Colloquially, it would mean to give too much jaw, as in speaking out of turn or, 'Blowing the Gaff.'

Gingerbread. (To take the gilt off the gingerbread, spoiling the look)
'Gingerbread' is the name given to the ornate carvings or dressings, of carved fretwork, applied to the stern or bows of a wooden ship. This would usually be over-painted, using a gilt or gold paint, for effect, and for elaborate show purposes. After a prolonged sea voyage, the paint would become worn or tarnished, leaving the decorative woodwork with a dull or flat look, and spoiling the effect. Hence the saying: 'Taking the gilt off the gingerbread'.

Give someone the slip. (To lose an unwanted follower.)
Relates to the practice of slipping the anchor-cable, when a speedy getaway was necessary. This might involve the ship making-way while the anchor was still overboard. (See also 'Cut and run.')

Glad rags. (Best dress or suit)
In maritime terms, it would mean to hoist your best set of sails, in other words, those sails without patches and repairs; usually used when a ship was about to be inspected, or during a 'Parade of sail', as part of a fleet or flotilla.

Glory hole. (A place to dump things not in use.)
A 'Strong room' on board ship, where items of some value could be securely stored. It also refers to a space or cupboard used by crewmembers, and left in a bit of a jumble.

Go ahead. (An order to carry on in the same way)
Usually an order given to the helmsman by the ship's engineer, instructing him to move on, or to go ahead with that which is already being done.

Go by the board. (See 'Board')

Grasp the nettle. (To tackle a difficulty, with courage)
'The Nettle' was a piece of rope, kept by the ship's bosun, which would be used to punish offenders.

Grog or 'Groggy' (Any form of alcohol, or to feel unwell)
'Grog' was named after Admiral Vernon, who, in about 1740, was nicknamed 'Old Grogham', after the 'grogham' cloth that was used to make the cloak he usually wore. Grog was a mixture of rum and water, named after the admiral; it was served to the ship's crew twice each day, making the uninitiated 'Groggy'.

Guff. (Empty talk, nonsense.)
A seafaring colloquialism, meaning unsupported or foolish talk.

Half cocked. (To speak too soon without considera-tion, to be only partly ready.)
When the hammer of a musket or flintlock was not completely pulled back into the firing position, the weapon was then 'Half cocked', and so would be unlikely to discharge completely, when attempting to fire the weapon. It can also mean a hurried action,

made by someone who was not aware of the consequences. Also means an unexpected discharge of a firearm.

Hand-over-fist. (To make rapid progress, with ease)
When an agile and experienced seaman can climb rapidly up ropes or rigging without using his legs, he would be said to be climbing 'Hand over fist'. Alternatively, when a rope is passed between both hands, inevitably, one hand would form a fist and a similar description would apply. It also means hauling rapidly on a rope and making good progress, with little effort.

Hang fire (To wait a minute, or stay one's hand)
A condition, which sometimes occurs, which causes a delay in the firing of a weapon. Or a delay, in the ignition of an explosive charge, which is unplanned.

Hard and fast. (Firm and unyielding, an unalterable rule)
A nautical expression: 'Hard', meaning immovable, 'Hard and fast', meaning a ship that is in dry dock, or been driven ashore and is unable to move. The word 'Hard' can also refer to a hard-standing, where boats can be loaded or stored.

Hard up. (Short of funds)
This describes two pulley blocks, which have been pulled together so closely (or hard up) that no further movement is possible. (See also Choc-a-block.)

Headway. (Making progress)
As a ship passes an item, such as a piece of flotsam or timber, (which would sometimes be deliberately thrown overboard, at the bow) and as the vessel travels onwards, eventually passing the item and leaving it behind in the ship's wake, it would be timed; from this, the ship's speed could be estimated. It would also be considered as 'making headway'. It also means to forge ahead or onwards. (See also 'Swinging the lead' and 'Knots')

Heavy weather. (A task made difficult through adverse conditions)
A nautical term for heavy rain, strong winds and rough seas, making progress difficult.

Heckle. (To disrupt or interfere during a speech, to deliberately annoy)
'Hetchel' or 'Hackle'. In maritime language, a hackle or heckle is a piece of machinery, used for teasing in, or inserting flax or caulking. 'To get one's hackles up', is taken, nowadays, to mean getting annoyed or angry.

High and dry. (Left deserted in a difficult situation)
Nautical phrase from the early 1900s, to describe a ship that has been left grounded, or left behind by the tide, for instance.

Hi-Jack. (Intention to rob, or to interrupt, or steal someone else's property or idea)

A 'Doxy's (lady of the night) call to a sailor, with every intention of stealing from him. After an initial embrace, the sailor would be hit over the head and then robbed. Alternatively, she might lure him into a house of ill-repute, from where, it was possible for him to be drugged, then dragged and dumped, in a drunken stupor. The next morning, he would wake, to find himself clad only in his underwear, and his money and clothes all gone. (See Figure 11)

Figure 11: 'Hi Jack'

Hold on too long. (To spend too long a time working on something, only to end up being too late for it to be useful)

A nautical phrase which refers to being too late in shortening sail, or holding on too long to the ship's top-sails, which would consequently cause some difficulty with the manoeuvrability of the ship.

Hookey or Hoaky. (To play truant)
A 19th century slang word meaning to go 'Absent without leave' (A.W.O.L.) This is not specifically a maritime word, but in maritime usage it is generally taken to mean someone at home, by the fireside, when they should be on board.

Hotshot. (An exceptionally able, expert, or important person)
Derives from the business of putting canon balls in a furnace to make them red hot, in order to temper them and to make them hard. It is also a term for a canon ball, that strikes an enemy canon head-on, or a bit too close for comfort, or that breaches a ship's side.

Hunky-dory. (All is well, or pleasurable)
Named after a street in Yokohama, Japan. A Street where sailors could obtain worldly pleasures, of many kinds.

Ill wind. (Misfortune, or bad luck)
Full quote: "It's an ill wind that blows no one any good, or that profits nobody."
An old nautical saying, probably millennia old, meaning, that if the wind doesn't suit your own ship, then it is bound to suit another. Colloquially, it is taken as meaning that one person's misfortune will usually benefit someone else.

Jack knife. (A folding pocketknife)
'Jack,' meaning sailor. The 'Jack-knife' is a clasp knife that closes into itself, or can be opened and locked, as needed. It would probably be tied to a lanyard to prevent it being dropped, and so, instantly available for use in an emergency i.e. for freeing ropes etc;

Jerry-built. (Something built roughly, with poor or insubstantial materials)
Corruption of 'Jury-built,' or perhaps 'Jury-rigged,' meaning makeshift or temporary. Often used, aboard ship, when knocking together chairs and /or tables for instance, or even makeshift repairs to masts or yards. As slang, the term 'Jury-rigged bum' means someone who is a bit of an odd job man. (See also Waster, Waister or even Dab-hand.)

Jump ship. (Leave without permission, or to desert a project)
To go absent without leave, or to desert a ship. (See also Hookey)

Junk. (Load of rubbish)
The name of a flat-bottomed, square-prowed vessel, made from cane or bamboo, and of Chinese or West Indian origin. It also refers to old rope or cable, cut into short lengths, used to make such things as Oakum. (Used for Caulking) In a modern navy, a 'Junk' would be classed as being inferior, in much the same way as old rope or cable would be referred to as rubbish. (See also: 'Money for old rope, and Corker/Cawker.')

Keel over. (Fall down, due to too much alcohol, or a faint)
A ship's keel is the main body of a ship, not including the superstructure. If the keel gets damaged in any way, i.e. in a storm, then it can tip-over, (Keel over) onto its side and be rendered useless. ('See also Beam-ends.')

Knots. (To travel at a rate of knots)
A Knot is a nautical measurement, a unit of distance, used in navigation. One knot equals: 2.025 yards, or one 'Sea mile' (See 'Log-book'.)

Knowing the ropes. (To be familiar with procedures)
The rigging of larger sailing vessels could comprise of miles of rope, separated into different lengths and thickness, for many uses. It was obligatory, for all crewmembers, to memorise the position of every rope - lives could well depend on it. In bad weather, especially on dark nights and in emergency conditions, it was imperative that every crewmember knew, instinctively, the position to go to, when the order for: 'Hands on,' was called. (See also 'learning the ropes')

Laid up. (Out sick, or out of service)
Referring to a ship, temporarily out of service, usually for repairs to be carried out. Making the vessel seaworthy would also include making good worn and frayed ropes. (See also 'At a loose end')

Lanyard (An item of dress, part of a uniform used by military personnel)

A piece of cord or hemp lit to smouldering stage in order to discharge a canon; this smouldering rope (or lanyard) was matched to the canon's 'touch hole' and would often be soaked in urine, and then dried, in order to make it smoulder and so burn for a longer period. In the 17th and 18th centuries, there was an expression known as 'Swinging the match'. This meant that the smouldering rope-end was being twirled around the person's head, to keep it glowing-red and in readiness for firing the canon.

This term also applies to a 'Match-lock', which was an old type of musket that had a match fixed adjacent to the touchhole, it would be placed next to the firing-pan, which held gunpowder as a primer. The person firing the musket would use the smouldering end of the match to touch, and so ignite the powder, in order to discharge the musket ball. Much later, matches, which were made from a sulphur base, were struck by using flints or coarse materials such as sandpaper; these were known as Vestas. A looped lanyard would also be used to release the hammer of a canon, or to hold a 'Jack knife', in order to save it from being accidentally dropped. (See 'Sideburns' and 'Sideboards')

Lash-up (Badly performed work)

To tie something down temporarily, usually in bad weather, when loose-lying equipment might otherwise be lost overboard. This temporary measure was termed as a 'Lash-up', which was expected to be put right at the earliest opportunity; if this did not come about, the job would remain a 'Lash-up. (See also 'Weathering the storm')

Learning the ropes. (Learning a new skill, or new procedure)
Apart from learning the location of every shipboard rope, (See also 'Know your ropes') sailors were required to learn, and be familiar with all types of knots, splices, and lashings, and to know where and when they were likely to be used. For their own good and for the good of their shipmates, apprentices, if they made mistakes, would often learn the hard way by feeling the rough end of a bosun's knotted-rope, across their backsides. (See also 'Grasping the nettle'

Let fly. (To verbally, and/or physically, lose one's temper)
Nautically, it means to let the sheets and sails of a sailing vessel fly out of control, so that they flapped against the masts and spars, directly downwind. This would be very bad seamanship, and would cause vessels to become out of control and losing 'Way'. (See also 'Making Way' and 'Three sheets to the wind')

Let the cat out of the bag. (Betray a secret)
The 'Cat', being the 'Cat-o-nine tails', (A specially designed whip with nine pieces of rope, sometimes with metal ends, and used for beatings) was usually kept in a felt, drawstring bag, and was brought out only to administer punishment.

Limelight. (To be in the forefront)
Most olden-day ships would use whale oil to replenish lighting fuel. By the 1800s, the whaling industry had been greatly reduced, and whale oil became scarce and expensive. Lighting, by the use of lime, was first used in 1825. It was used extensively as a lighting agent aboard ships, because it gave out an intense white-light, this was obtained by heating a cylinder of lime, which formed an 'oxy-hydrogen' flame. At that time, a similar system was used in theatres and houses of pleasure. (Putting important characters, and the like, in the' limelight')

Listless. (Tired and apathetic)
Nautically, it means that a ship lies becalmed, or so called in the Doldrums, (See also 'Doldrums') and therefore not able to 'list', (to move one way or another.) In other words, the ship is classed as 'Listless'.

Logbook. (Record of a ship's working life. Vehicle ownership)
In olden days of sail, in order to judge the speed and progress of a sailing ship, a piece of wood or a small log would be thrown overboard, (ahead of the ship.) Its progress was timed as the ship and log passed each other, which would give a general indication of the ship's speed, and would be calculated against the actual length of the vessel. To get a more accurate reading, knots would be tied at measured distances (probably in fathoms at 6 feet intervals) along a rope attached to the wood, then timed as it passed by the ship. This is

where the words 'Logbook', and 'Knots' (as in sea miles) come from. (See also 'Fathom')

Loggerheads. (Argumentative, or violently opposed to someone or something)
This is a maritime name for a projectile, consisting of two canon balls linked together by an iron bar, made in such a way as to effect maximum casualties and much damage to an enemy ship. It was also capable of 'demasting' an enemy ship, in much the same way, as 'Chain shot' would do. 'Loggerheads' was also the name of the wooden 'bitts' in the stern of a whaling boat, on which the harpoon line was held. (When harpoons were launched by hand). (See Figure 12.)

Long shot. (Taking a chance, or a gamble)
Nautically speaking, in days long gone, the accuracy of a ship's guns was always suspect. It was largely left to the skills of the 'Master of guns' or the 'Gunnery officer' to calculate the required range. This was a difficult task, especially when there was a considerable distance between the canon and its target. On most occasions, it was considered to be more by luck than judgement when the canon found its target; in other words, it was 'a long shot'.

Loom. (Overshadow)
The loom of the land is that which projects above the horizon. The vista and size of which can be exaggerated by the refraction of light, which makes the land seem visibly closer than it is.

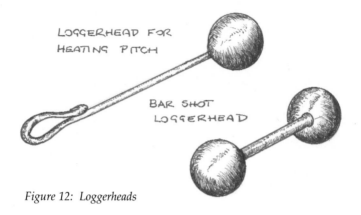

LOGGERHEAD FOR
HEATING PITCH

BAR SHOT
LOGGERHEAD

Figure 12: Loggerheads

Loopholes. (The way out of a situation, often having legal connections)

Generally, 'loopholes' were formed in the ship's 'castle walls', so that canons or small arms could be fired at the enemy, or potential boarding parties, and at the same time would give partial cover to those firing the guns. These smallish apertures gave some personal protection from enemy fire. Loopholes were also formed in a ship's bulkheads and hatches.

Loose canon. (An out of control situation, which could result in disaster)

Enormous canons were sometimes used on fighting ships, and it was possible for their tethers to break, after firing, by recoil. This would leave the canon loose and out of control, which could cause loss of life and great damage to the ship itself.

Loose ends. (Temporarily unoccupied)
Nautically, when rope ends become unravelled they are called 'Loose-ends'. (See also 'Fag ends') When a crew member was found to be idle, or have very little to do, he might well be given the job of going around checking the ropes, and whipping, splicing, or repairing any 'loose ends', so keeping him gainfully employed.

Lump sum. (Full payment)
A dockside, or shipside worker, would be paid a lump sum of money on completion of a job of work. Also referred to as 'Cash in hand'. These workers would be described as working 'On the lump.' A similar title might be given to labourers on building sites, employed as temporary workers, on a daily basis.

Mainstay. (An important and reliable person)
The 'Mainstay' is part of a ship's standing rigging which prevents the masts from collapsing; it also carries the largest and the most-important sails. The 'Stays' that control sideways movement are called 'Shrouds'. It could be said that 'Mainstays' are the most important part of a ship's rigging. (See 'Shrouds') (See Figure 13.)

Make and mend. (Recycle, make something useful out of very little)
Could be considered a seaman's 'half holiday'. This term originates from the custom of giving a ship's crew time off whilst at sea. It might well be just one after-

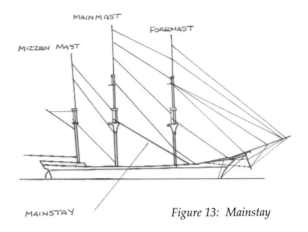

MIZZEN MAST
MAINMAST
FOREMAST
MAINSTAY

Figure 13: Mainstay

noon a week to carry out repairs and washing of clothing, or dealing with any other personal equipment, especially when replacements would be impossible to get, until the ship reached port.

Make way. (Move aside)
Once a ship has been released from her moorings and is floating free, a senior officer will give the order to 'Make way', meaning to move forward, or make headway. It also describes any forward movement of the vessel.

Making a rod for one's own back. (To make things difficult for oneself)
It was customary for crew-members, awaiting punishment, to make or fashion their own instrument of punishment: a cane, stick, or a Cat-o-nine tails. They may be given a length of rope and ordered to splice, strand or plait it into the nine tails, leaving enough rope to

form a rope handle. In the event that this task was not completed satisfactorily, they would be given extra lashings as further punishment.

Match. (A person or thing exactly alike, or corresponding one to another)
This would be a piece of cord or hemp, which would be lit and allowed to smoulder, and used to fire a cannon or matchlock musket; this was done by matching the smouldering cord to the 'touchhole' of the canon or musket. This rope or cord would often be soaked in urine and dried, which was a way of making it smoulder for a longer time. Sometimes, the match (firing mechanism) was sited adjacent to the touchhole, close to the 'hammer' and near to the firing pan. (See 'Flash in the pan') Gun powder in the pan was ignited by the match, this, in turn, would ignite the powder in the gun, or cannon's muzzle, to fire the ball. Later, wooden matches called 'Vestas', which had sulphur matchheads and were lit by striking them on stone or course material, were used for the purpose. (See sideburns and sideboards. Also see lanyard.)

Mate. (A friend or fellow worker)
A rank, immediately below that of the ship's master, who is known as the 'First mate'. Certainly of maritime origin and taken from the old English word 'Gemetta', meaning the 'sharer of food'. Today it would mean to share a loyal friendship, or to be an assistant to a skilled worker.

Maul. (Subjected to rough treatment)
This is a heavy wooden or metal hammer used for caulking. A wide, blunt chisel is used to press the 'oakum' between the wooden planks of the ship, and to hold it in position, while the 'Maul' is used for hammering the chisel in order to drive the caulking firmly into position. It also means to engage in battle, which is possibly why we use the word 'Maul', colloquially, as an attack on someone or something.

Mayday. (Emergency call for help)
Comes from the French language, from the word 'M'aidez', meaning: 'Help me!' pronounced 'Mayday.' Universally recognized as an urgent call for help, in much the same way as S.O.S. ('save our souls' or 'save our ships') that would mean all persons at risk. Also used in all arms of the services, as well as private use.

Mayonnaise (Salad dressing)
Not a true maritime word, but it was 'coined' by the French naval officer *Duc de Richelieu*, when, following a successful battle against the British navy in 1756, off the Majorcan capital 'Mahon', a banquet was given in his honour. A new recipe, used as a dressing, was concocted using eggs, vinegar, oil and pepper, blended with salt and mustard. It was so much enjoyed that they named it after his great victory, and called it *'Mahon naise'*, or as we now know it, *'Mayonnaise'*.

Miss the boat. (Too late to be of any use)
If a crew-member turned up late, after a scheduled

shore leave, he would miss his lift back to his ship. He would then be regarded as being 'absent without leave', and in serious trouble.

Money for old rope. (Making an easy fortune, from a very small amount)
In days long past, the ship's Purser, as well as crewmembers, would keep all the odd ends of rope and take them ashore, to sell. Frayed rope-ends would be of little value aboard ship, but ashore they could be sold as wicks for candles, or plaited together to make soft toys, on which, they would make profit.

Moonlighting. (A second job, other than a fulltime day-job, which is usually against company policy)
Originally, of seafaring origin, referring to smugglers landing 'contraband', usually taking place at night, hence the term 'Moonlighting'.

My eye. (Unbelievable nonsense)
(See 'Turning a blind eye')

Nailing one's colours to the mast. (Resolute, loyal, and unwavering)
Sailing vessels, and more modern ships, usually fly their national flag from the masthead. If these flags got shot away during battle, they would be replaced and fixed to the mast in any way possible. (Using nails if nothing more suitable was to hand) Should flags not be replaced, the enemy could construe it as a sign of surrender. False colours would usually be the domains of

pirates; they would fly any available flag until they were ready to attack, then they would raise their own 'Black Flag', or the 'Skull and Crossbones' (See also 'Union Jack')

Nautical. (Sailor like)
The Greek word for 'Ship' was 'Naus' and from that we get 'Nautical', 'Nautilus', and 'Nausea'. (Another word for sickness or seasickness) The word 'Naus' then passed into Latin as 'Navis', from where, words such as 'Navy', 'Navigate' and 'Navvy' came from.

Nipper. (A young person)
Naval slang for a young boy. Anchor cables, made from hemp, were wound or taken up by a 'Capstan'. This long, heavy wet-rope would sometimes become difficult to reel in, so keeping the rope moving would be the job of the young lads ('Nippers') or apprentices. This would be achieved by easing it away from the 'Messenger,' (a rope feeder) probably using wooden levers to help ease the rope or cable through. A 'Nipper's job would be to secure the 'Messenger' to the ropes or cables. These young lads had to be quick off the mark, agile and dextrous, otherwise it could be a very dangerous task to perform, especially if they should get their hands or feet tangled up with the taut or stretched cable. (See Figure 14)

Nitty-Gritty. (Basic details, or realities of a matter)
In naval terms, 'Nitty' means a disagreement, row, quarrel, or even a noise; followed by 'Gritty', a name that comes originally from eastern counties of England,

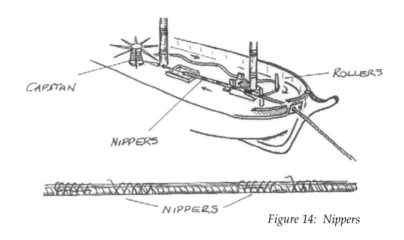

Figure 14: Nippers

where it is the name used for a sea crab that drags itself along the seabed. *'Nitty'* or *'nits'* is also a name for the eggs of young head lice, which, when discovered amongst a ship's crew, would need urgent treatment. It has been suggested by some that *'Nitty-Gritty'* is a politically incorrect term, somehow connected with the slave trade, although no evidence of these claims have been found.

No great shakes. (Not much good)

As barrels on board ship became empty, they would be lifted, and shaken to ensure that all the contents had been used. Once this had been established, and to save on valuable storage space, each barrel would be taken apart then tied and stored flat, ready for reassembling when needed for further use. Once the barrels had been emptied and taken apart, they were not of much use, so of *'no great shakes'*.

No room to swing a cat. (Not much room to move)
Space on board ship could be very cramped, so in order to administer a flogging with the 'Cat-o-nine tails', the punishment was likely to be carried out on deck, with the victim tied to part of the ship's super-structure, or even a canon. (See 'Swinging the cat and 'over a barrel')

Nous. (Everyday slang, meaning to have knowledge)
This word probably originated from the Medit-erranean area. It occurs frequently in maritime litera-ture, meaning to be very knowledgeable. (*Pronounced as one would the words 'house' or 'mouse'.*)

Oars ('Put one's oar in', meaning to meddle, or inter-fere)
At one time, this was purely a maritime term, which has permeated into everyday English language. In maritime usage, it just means to put or to dip the oars into the water to propel a boat. The order to 'Rest on your oars' (or just 'Oars') would mean to lie across them and to stop rowing until further instructions, which might be to do the opposite of that which is hap-pening at the time, or to pause after some successful negotiating, and take rest.

Odds and Sods. (Odd bits and pieces)
Not particularly an exclusive, naval expression, although it does refer to extra people, on board ship, for the purpose of making up numbers that were need-ed for certain mundane tasks. This would release the

skilled sailors in order to carry out more important rolls. The expression *'Odds and Sods'* is usually used to show a mariner's contempt for crewmembers that are not real or regular seaman. Another name for such people would be *'Idlers and Waisters'* (*See also 'Waister'*)

Off the wall. (Unorthodox, unconventional)
This refers to a vessel that is floating free, having been released, or disconnected from a permanent anchorage, from a dock or harbour. So, in slang terms, it is referred to as being 'Off the wall'.

Oil on troubled waters. (To calm down a situation or argument)
It is a scientific fact, that when oil is poured onto heavy seas it can form an 'oil slick', which helps to decrease wave violence. In heavy weather, oil bags would be hung over the ship's side and allowed to drain into the sea; this would help to prevent the waves from breaking over the ship.

Old man. (Man in charge, Boss, Captain, or even father)
This expression is usually made out of respect, or affection. In maritime terms, it refers to the 'skipper' of a vessel.

Oldster. (An older and experienced person)
In naval language, this refers to a midshipman who has four or more years of service and experience. (The opposite of 'Youngster')

On an even keel. (All is going well, in a stable condition)
A term used when all cargo and provisions have been loaded, stored and balanced correctly, so that the vessel is steady and stable, or 'on an even keel'.

On the beach. (Out of action - retired from the sea)
(See 'Swallow the anchor')

On the nail. (Cash paid 'Up front' or when requested)
(See 'Pay on the nail')

On strike. (Making a Protest, by withdrawing manpower, until a fair deal is agreed upon)
This saying has its maritime roots dating back some 200 years, when life at sea could be particularly cruel and unjust, and when harsh punishment would be handed out to offenders. Seamen sometimes got together, to protest about conditions, and would 'Strike the sails'; this was meant as an indication that they would lower them, to prevent the ship from leaving port, until a settlement had been agreed with the ship's owners or their managers and captain. (See also 'Round Robin')

Out of the blue. (Totally, unexpected happening)
Meaning a big change in the weather, or change in circumstances. A 'squall' could occur at the most inappropriate time, going from a stiff breeze under a blue sky, and unexpectedly into a heavy storm. If a ship

happened to be under full sail at the time, it could well lead to a disaster, with loss of life, or even loss of the ship itself.

Out on a limb. (Isolated, stranded, at a disadvantage or at risk)
A seaman, who might have, hurriedly, climbed out too far onto the 'Yardarm', in order to work on sails, i.e. releasing or securing them, (possibly in an emergency and without a safety harness) would be in great danger when trying to return to safety, and would be classed as being 'Out on a limb'.

Over a barrel (Caught in a trap with nowhere to turn)
This expression originates from the old days of sail, when a seaman, facing punishment, would be 'spread-eagled' and tied to a gun barrel to receive his punishment, which would probably be a flogging with the 'cat o nine tails'. (See 'Let the cat out of the bag' and 'No room to swing a cat')

Overboard. (To act excitedly or to exaggerate by showing off)
To 'Jump overboard', or 'jump ship', for reasons unknown, very possibly into stormy seas. Colloquially, it refers to an unreasonable reaction, by a person, over something relatively minor. Or be over enthusiastic and go too far.

Overhaul. (To repair, put right, or to service a piece of equipment)

Originally, this was a naval expression meaning to examine and repair or service, when necessary, any onboard equipment. This would include the overhauling and easing and slackening of ropes, on the 'Block and tackle', in order to release tension or to free the ropes in a 'Choc-a-block' (cramped) situation. (See 'Choc-a-block')

Overwhelmed. (To be overcome by emotion, or physical attack)

Nautically, it means to capsize, or to roll over.

Packet. (A small, wrapped package, also something costing a lot of money)

A '*Packet*' is a small sailing boat, which was used to carry mail and goods, from ship to ship, around a port. It was probably the quickest way of transporting goods in a seaport area, but not necessarily the most economical. So, to send goods and mail in this way would '*Cost a packet*'. (See Figure 15)

Parting shot. (Usually a final cutting remark or comment)

This is a metaphoric term regarding the firing of weapons; especially the final shot that would finish off the enemy. The original reference to this term was recorded in 1818 by John McLeod, who was a ship's surgeon on HMS ALCESTE, in his narrative: *A Voyage To The Yellow Sea*.

Figure 15: Packet

Paunch. (Large, protruding belly, usually of someone living the good life)
A heavy mat made up from strands of rope, used to protect spars and rigging from chafing, especially when the vessel is rolling heavily, due to the sea's swell. (See also 'Bolster')

Pickled. (Food preserved by pickling, or someone who is drunk from alcohol)
It has been rumoured that this word originates from the days of Admiral Lord Nelson. Although there are records of it being used long before Nelson's death in 1805, when he was placed in a barrel of brandy, to preserve his corpse, which was being shipped back to England. ('Nelson's blood', reputedly, was rum, but in fact it was brandy.')

Pigeon holed. (A basic filing system. To assign a person/thing to a certain category)
Nautically, it refers to the square holes in the 'Drumhead' situated at the top of a capstan, into which the 'Capstan bars' are slotted, in order to wind it up.

Pillar to post. (Pushed or propelled from one place to another)
Originally expressed as being 'Careening from pillar to post', then corrupted to 'Careering from pillar to post'. 'Careening' means to haul a ship onto its side, using tackles, for repairs and cleaning of the ship's hull and bottom. The ship would be secured between two points, probably from one of the ship's pillars, to a convenient post. Pillars are the vertical columns of wood supporting the decks and beams of a vessel, also supporting the ship's framework across the vertical plane.

Pinch. (Something difficult, but manageable - with luck. A small amount.)
To 'Pinch-up' is to sail a vessel as close as possible to the wind, so close that her sails would 'shiver and shake'. The vessel would then only just scrape through a manoeuvre, or would turn and possibly lose some speed. (See 'Shivers')

Piping hot. (Steaming hot)
Whistle calls were the normal way of life, on board ship; they indicated the many orders to be carried out during the ship's daily life. These were usually made via the *'Bosun's Call.'* (Or pipe) At the end of a working

day, for instance, they would be used to *'Pipe down'*. (An order for the crew to retire for the night, and it also meant to keep quiet) To *'Pipe up'* would mean the opposite. The *'Pipe'* (or Bosun's call) was also used to welcome dignitaries on board ship, such as: Heads of State, Royalty, and perhaps, female guests. *'Piping to orders,'* is used on board for many tasks, especially when at sea and facing strong winds, when, the sound of a pipe would be more likely to carry further than the human voice would. *'Piping hot'* would be a term used on larger ships, where the mess decks would be big, holding larger numbers of crew. Following a piped message, meals would either be collected or delivered to the mess deck, from the galley, and would be considered to be 'Piping hot'. (Equivalent to shouting: "Come and get it!") (See Figure 16)

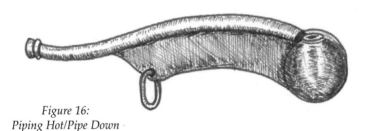

Figure 16:
Piping Hot/Pipe Down

Plane (or 'Plain') Sailing. (An uncomplicated, easy-going task)

This is a part of navigation that treats a ship's course as a geometric angle, using the latitude, eastings and westings, for reference points. Colloquially, 'Plane sailing' means that a task is relatively simple, and almost impossible to make a mistake in the execution of it.

Plumb the depths. (To go to the extreme in carrying out a search for something, i.e. a way out of a problem - mentally or physically)
This is where the word 'Plummet' comes from, also 'Plum-line'. In the olden days of sail, a 'Plumber' was a person who specialized in making lead weights and probably lead pipes as well. Lead weights, tied to cords, were dropped over the side of the ship; tallow or grease would be pressed into the recess, in the bottom of the weight, in order to pick up soft material, such as sand, from the sea bed, and to establish whether or not the ship might be in danger of running aground. It would also be used to calculate the depth of water or the draught of a ship. Ties would be added to the rope, at certain distances, e.g. at fathom distances. (See also 'Swinging the lead')

Plumb line. (Used in most of the construction trades to ensure a straight line)
(See also 'Plumb the depths')

Pooped. (Tired or exhausted)
A ship, running before a heavy sea, could well be overtaken by a powerful wave, which could break over the 'Poop-deck' and cause flooding. This would make tiring work for the crew, who would be battling to keep the ship from sinking. After a long and arduous fight to save the vessel, the crew would be well and truly 'Pooped' or exhausted.

Posh. (Smart, stylish, associated with upper class)
This word (or description) reputedly goes back to the old P&O days and the time of the RAJ in India, and the British Empire. Before the Suez Canal was opened in 1869, travel abroad was mostly done by ship, via the Cape of Good Hope, off South Africa.

Travelling to India, the upper classes, and military officers and their wives, would invariably seek, on the outward journey, cabin accommodation on the port side of the ship. This would be the coolest place to be, and would have portholes for ventilation. On the homeward journey, however, the opposite would apply; so top class accommodation would then be on the starboard side. All return tickets for these passengers would have 'P.O.S.H.' stamped on them, meaning that they would be travelling portside out, (which is on the left looking forward) and the starboard side when returning home. The poorer classes, and the military rank and file, would be accommodated, less comfortably, on the opposite side, each way of the journey. Hence the word POSH which meant: Port Outward, Starboard Home. (It has been said that P&O had never actually used this stamp on their travel tickets, and that this is a later association rather than the true origin.)

Pram. (Perambulator, baby carriage)
Nautically, a 'Pram' is a small, flat-bottomed boat, used for short journeys from ship to shore; the main purpose being to ferry people or light cargo. This, it would seem, is why a small boat of this size was reminiscent of a baby carriage, which is also known as a 'Pram'.

The 'Pram', nautically, was also used as a small sailing vessel, which was armed to defend the coastal regions of France and Holland, during Napoleonic times.

Put about. (To pass on information, to spread rumour)
Nautically, it means to turn around, to put a ship on the opposite tack and so change direction. (See 'Tack')

Quarantine. (In isolation)
A word which applied to sailing ships, when passengers, or crew, were suspected of having been exposed to a contagious disease, and where there was risk of the disease being spread. The ship would then be put into isolation. (Under quarantine) The word 'Quarantine' comes from the Latin word for 'Forty', which was the expected period of time, in days, for a contagious disease to be confirmed and the period of time the ship would be 'under quarantine', before being allowed to enter port.

Quid. (Slang name for £1 or one pound sterling)
The word 'Quid', a corruption of 'Cud' (as in 'chewing the cud') refers to a plug of chewing tobacco. (See also 'Eat my hat') Sailors, on wooden ships, were unlikely to be allowed to smoke pipes because of the risk of fire, so they would chew tobacco instead. All tobacco products could well be used as a form of currency, hence the saying: "Lend me a quid". Tobacco, in those days, was used on board ship, between crew-members, so the term: "Lend me a quid" was actually asking for a loan of tobacco; unlike today when it would mean asking

for the loan of a pound coin. Even today, cigarettes and tobacco are used in prison and the armed services, as a form of currency for gambling or bartering purposes.

Rack and ruin. (Destruction, derelict. or bankrupt)
Originally spelt 'Wrack' and is, in fact, another version of 'Wreck'. Nautically, it means: driven ashore and brought to a state of disrepair; or otherwise something, 'In rack and ruin', usually referred to the ruination of an object or person, which had been brought about by neglect.

Rate of knots. (Speed at which a ship travels)
A nautical term from the time when distance, and speed of a ship, was measured by *'knots'*. These knots would be tied along the length of a rope or cord, at measured distances, probably a fathom (six feet) apart. (See *'Fathom'*) The rope or cord would then be tied to a suitable floating-object, such as a piece of wood, which would then be held at one end, and the free end dropped overboard. By counting the number of knots as the rope floated past the vessel, and using the actual length of the ship as a gauge, it would be possible to calculate the speed at which the ship was travelling. (A knot is also known as a 'Nautical mile')   (*See also* *'Knots' and 'Log book'*)

Rest on one's oars. (To take a breather)
After a spell of heavy rowing, a break could well be called for; the boat's crew would lay their oars horizontally, in line to the water, and then rest themselves by leaning across them. (See also *'Oars'*)

Ringleader. (A person seemingly in charge of a given situation, often illicitly)
Sometimes known as a *'Round Robin'*, in other words a circular petition against authority, where no one particular person is seen to be the leader or instigator. Originally used by sailors when making a formal request, or protest, as a way of avoiding being branded a mutineer. (*See also 'Strike'*)

Round Robin. (A circular course, as with a letter. To operate in a rotational manner, i.e. in a tournament)
The earliest dates for this term go back to the 16th century, when it was regarded as being along the lines of 'sly dog'. Its use as a Naval term was recorded in 1730; when it was a form of petition; complainants would sign their names in a circle, in order to disguise the first person that signed it. This would prevent the ringleader from being discovered, as in those days, mutiny was a hanging offence. It is not surprising that seamen so much favoured this way of making their grievances known, especially as punishments, in those times, were so cruelly harsh. (See also 'Strike')

Rover. (A wanderer)
This is taken from the Dutch language 'Zee-rover', meaning: 'Sea Rover' or 'Sea Robber'; a name that was given to: 'Pirates', Vagabonds', Privateers', and 'Buccaneers'. It also means to wander or move about aimlessly.

Rule of thumb. (A rule for general guidance, based on experience rather than theory)
A practical, rather than an accurate measurement, used by sailors who found reading and writing difficult, and before the use of more efficient ways of calculation. In other words, it was a 'Guesstimate', or a rough idea of the general size or length of an item. It is also a measurement for a tot of whiskey, which was sometimes referred to as a 'finger of whisky'. At one time, there used to be an unwritten law that a man could chastise his spouse by beating her with a stick, providing it was no thicker that his thumb!

Sail under false colours. (Pretence, appearing to be someone or something different from the apparent)
A hypocrite for instance. Enemy ships and pirates would fly false flags or colours, in order to deceive others into believing that they were something other than they really were. A pirate ship, for instance, would fly the flag of a previously, plundered vessel, in order to fool their target into believing they were friendly. Once they had sailed within canon range, the false colours would be '*struck*' (taken down) and replaced with their true colours, probably the black flag or the skull and crossbones. (*See also 'Nail one's colours to the mast'*)

Salt. (A long-serving and experienced sailor. 'Worth his salt')
Often referred to as a 'Shellback', because of his reputation for having 'barnacles' and 'limpets' growing on his back, just like his ship would have after a long sea

voyage. A 'Salt' (or sailor) would also be expected to have salt in his blood, and is probably where the saying: 'Worth his salt', comes from. All this would also earn him the title of an 'Old salt'. (*See also 'Crossing the line*)

Scandalize. (To spread rumours, create problems for others)
Although this expression is not of nautical origin, seamen use it extensively; the word is firmly in place in the maritime language, used at sea. It means: to deliberately set a ship's sails and spars in disarray by setting them in different directions, with sails hanging loose as a sign of mourning for the death of a shipmate, or a sign that there is something seriously wrong with the ship itself. (See also 'Strike')

Scrambled egg. (Gold embellishments)
A nickname, given by the rank and file, for the gold embellishments on the cap, sleeves, and epaulets of ranking officers' uniforms, because of its resemblance to scrambled eggs! The nickname 'Brass hats' means virtually the same thing; senior, naval officers, who held the rank of commander, and above, wore these. Another nickname for an officer is 'Big-Wig', possibly referring to the powdered wigs, worn, in days past, by officers and many high officials.

Scraper. (For removing waste, and tacky or difficult material)
A 'Scraper' is a triangular piece of metal with two or three sharp edges, used for scraping the ship's sides and decks after 'Caulking'.   It was also the name for the three-cornered, tricorn hat, sometimes worn by officers. (See also 'Bowing and scraping')

Scraping the barrel. (To be reduced to one's last resources)
Clearing out the refuse, or last dregs, from the bottom of used wooden-barrels, would be done with a triangular piece of metal, known as a 'scraper'.   Hence the saying: "Scraping the bottom of the barrel". (See 'Scraper')

Scratch my back and I'll scratch yours. ('Do me a favour and I'll return it')
On long sea voyages, punishment, to crewmembers, happened with some regularity, as seamen would, inevitably, break rules and regulations. Punishment was usually a flogging and would be administered, mainly, by fellow seamen; therefore it made sense to bargain, one with the other, to go easy with the flogging.   When the punishment was reversed, then the favour would be returned.   Scratches would be cuts and marks across the back, as a result of the flogging.

Scrub around it. (Forget it! or avoid it)
Taken from the task of scrubbing the decks with *'Pumice'* or *'Sandstone'*. An order to: "scrub round it", meant that any obstruction, which was difficult to move, was to be avoided. Another name for *'Pumice'* (A bi-product of lava and sandstone) was 'holystone', named so, because men kneeling to scrub the decks resembled men praying. (*See also 'Bible'*)

Seize. (To grab an opportunity or to take possession of someone/something, forcibly)
To fasten, or attach together, any parts of two ropes. Or to join the rope ends by *'Whipping'*, (binding or plaiting) to form an eye, when working other ropes.

Sewn up. (A job completed)
Meaning that all is well and *'Squared away'* aboard ship, and that sails are *'Clewed up'*. If someone died when the ship was a good distance away from shore, they would be sewn into their hammock before being buried at sea. Superstition had it that bad luck would come to any other seaman using the dead man's hammock. (*See also 'Clewed up' and 'Shrouds'*)

Shake a leg or show a leg. (Get out of bed, wake up, or make a start.)
In days long-gone, to ensure that crew-members, due to go 'on watch', were awake and alert, the Bosun, or the Bosun's mate, would move amongst the sleeping crew-members, shouting, to get them up for work. This is still part of today's language: to get people to hurry themselves or to wake up. At one time, some

females went to sea with their men folk, and when the order to 'Show a leg' was bawled out, the women would stick out a stockinged-leg, in order to be identified as 'ladies' who were under the bed covers; they would then be allowed to stay there until the men were up, dressed and ready, to report to their posts. In these more 'Communal lodgings', there must have been many mix-ups, and the so-called 'ladies' were probably not as modest as perhaps they should have been; as a result, there were unwanted pregnancies. (*See also 'Son of a gun'*)

Shakes. (A couple of shakes, a short time.)
This is a name used, by shipwrights and carpenters, to describe splits in timbers, where the grain becomes separated. Storing empty barrels aboard ship, took up a great deal of space, so they would be taken apart, by separating the staves, then tied in bundles, and stacked neatly away. When needed, they would be reassembled, and would often be found to have a stave or two, rotted, or missing from the bundle; this meant someone would have to hold, in position, the partly assembled barrel, while another went off to fetch more staves, which they'd have to be quick about. Hence, the call: '*Back in a couple of shakes.*'

Shanty. (Songs, sung by sailors, while hauling ropes; often made up as they went along)
There are three spellings: Shanty, Chanter, and Chantey, all of which are correct, depending on one's point of view. '*Chantey*' is taken from the French,

'chanter', to *'Sing-out* or to *'Chatter'*. The late Stan Hugill, an expert in most things maritime, said that as far as he was concerned the word spelt, *'Shanty'*, is correct. This, he said, referred to the old 'Shanty towns' that grew up alongside the seaports, especially in North America, where Negro slaves were used to load and unload ships' cargoes. Many of the basic native-chants, sung by these slaves, were heard by ships' crews, and were adopted by them, as working-songs or rhythms. These chants would then be used aboard their own vessels. That is why the words of many such shanties were indecipherable; especially when taken from words or sounds used by the slaves, which would have made little or no sense to the other listeners. Once a ship was completely loaded or unloaded, these temporary shelters housing the slaves, called 'Shanty towns', would be dismantled. They would then be carried, or pushed and pulled, to the next port of work, where the slaves would re-assemble their lodgings, and so create another *'Shanty town'*. (*See Figure 17*)

Figure 17: Shanty

Shape up (Show promise, make good progress or else get out)

A navigator would be instructed to, *'shape a course'*, for the ship to follow; if he didn't prove to be sufficiently skilled in the shaping of this course, he would be ordered to, *'shape up'*, (improve) or *'ship out'*, (get out). Generally speaking, this term could apply to anyone found to be not skilled enough, or even too lazy, to perform a prescribed task satisfactorily.

Sheets. (Three sheets to the wind, meaning, not mentally acute, usually due to an excess of alcohol)

Often, people think of the ship's *'sheets'* as being the sails, they are, in fact, the sails' control-ropes or chains, which are attached to the bottom corners of the sails' 'clews', which are situated at the bottom corners of the sails, in order to hold them in place. (See 'Clewed-up). If sails were loose or incorrectly raised, with the sheets (ropes) flying free, the ship would roll about and become unstable and difficult to steer. Colloquially, it refers to a person who is rendered incapable, due to over indulgence of alcohol.

Ship shape. (Neat and tidy)

This originates from Bristol and the Bristol docks. The river Avon was renowned for the mud and silt, washed up by the tides, so it was imperative for locally-built boats and ships to be shaped in a certain way, in order for them to be capable of sitting on the muddy bottom, when the tide was low; otherwise, vessels would be in danger of rolling onto their sides. (See also 'Bristol fashion', and 'Beam ends'.)

Shivers. (A quick trembling-movement of the body, due to shock, fear, cold. etc)

Probably out of place here, as it is not necessarily an everyday naval-term. However, there is a well-known expression that is of maritime origin: 'Shiver me timbers'. When a sail starts to flutter, or to shake severely, especially when steered too close to the wind, it can make the vessel move erratically, which could well cause the wind to spill out of her sails, and throw the ship off course. (See also 'Shakes')

Shove off. (Move off - get out of the way)

Nautically, it means to push or to 'clear off', as with a small boat, by hand or by boat hook. Colloquially, it means to get going, or to move away from someone's presence.

Shroud. (Garment for clothing a body to make ready for burial)

Nautically speaking, the shrouds are the ropes that form part of a ship's *'Standing rigging'*, which supports the masts and topmasts, giving them lateral support, in much the same way as the *'Stays'* give fore and aft support. There seems to be no logical explanation for this nautical word to be used in connection with a burial garment, unless it suggests covering the masts. (*See also 'Lanyards' - See Figure 18*)

Sideboards. (See 'Sideburns')

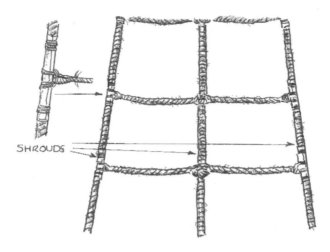

Figure 18: Shrouds

Sideburns. (Hair grown down the side of a man's face)

When a Royal Marine or a Musketeer fired a flintlock rifle, it was quite possible that some of the igniting gunpowder, held in the pan or priming dish, when fired, would flare out sideways, scorching and burning that side of the face. To help protect themselves from the burns, they would grow hair down the sides of their faces - although this rarely worked. Some protection could be given by sliding a piece of board, under their hats, to the side nearest the gun. These were called 'Sideboards' (*See Figure 19*)

Skyscrapers. (Unusually high buildings)

These were triangular sails, usually used in pairs, on square-rigged sailing ships. They were set at the highest-possible point of the mast, just beneath the

SIDEBURNS

Figure 19:
Sideboards/Sideburns

'button'. (The place where all ropes (sheets) and sails terminate) On very large ships, this could be a hundred or more feet high, so high, that they looked as though they were scraping the sky. They were used, as a temporary measure, to gain speed, when winds were light and time was of the essence. (*See Figure 20*)

Slackers. (Those people who don't 'Pull their weight'.)
This expression supposedly comes from Nova Scotia and the Canadian navy. This relates to times when work on board ship would be 'Slacked off', especially when in a homeport, and especially during war years, when sailors needed respite after long journeys at sea.

Slip. (To escape. To give away a secret by letting it 'slip')
Nautically, it would mean to release a ship's inboard mooring-line, so that the vessel floats clear of the shore.

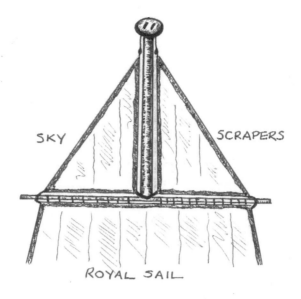

Figure 20: Skyscrapers

Metaphorically it means to leave secretly, or to give someone the slip. (*See also 'Cut and run' and 'Give someone the slip*)

Slush fund. (Profits put aside for emergencies)
The ship's cook would store oil, grease and fat, which accumulated on the mess decks and galley, until the ship put into a convenient port. The Purser would then sell it on to pay towards the manufacture of candles, for use on board ship, or to put towards the ship's expenses. Hence the term, 'Slush fund,' or 'Slosh fund'. Another related term is, 'Slushy' or 'Slosh', names used for the ship's cook.

Snotty. (Derogatory slang-title, for someone who seems unpleasant, angry, easily irritated)

This was a naval slang for a 'Midshipman' (trainee officer) without maritime experience; they were sent to sea to train as potential officers, and would have been subsidised by rich parents or sponsors. These young lads were called 'Snottie's', due to their habit of wiping their noses on their coat sleeves, either from cold, or fear, especially in battle conditions. Traditionally, it has been reported that Admiral Lord Nelson ordered large buttons to be sewn, onto midshipmen's tunic-sleeves, in an attempt to dissuade them from this practice.

Sod's law. (An unexpected, coincidental happening, usually of an unfortunate nature)

Used in maritime language, taken from the word '*Sodom*', meaning a wicked or depraved place, which, no doubt, sailors will have come across many times during their travels. The saying would be incorporated in many coincidental, or inexplicable happenings that occurred on board ships, especially in the olden days when superstition, amongst seamen, was rife.

Son of a gun. (A term used, jocularly, for a likeable, affectionate character)

In days long gone, before it became superstitious to allow females to go to sea as crewmembers, some women would accompany their men folk on long sea voyages. (See also 'Shake', or 'show a leg'.) Inevitably, pregnancies would occur. Space, especially on warships, was very limited. Giving birth, would only be possible in the small spaces between the canons, on the gun decks, or behind a smaller area covered by sheeting or canvas. Male children had to be registered in the ship's log, as potential seamen. Female children were not seen to be important, so did not need to be listed! Male babies would be known, individually, as 'A son of a gun', because there would often be some doubt over the child's parentage.

Soundings (Getting opinions, before taking action)

When testing the depths of shallow water, at sea, a lead weight (or other heavy material) would be tied to a line, and dropped overboard. 'Tallow' was smeared on the end of the weight, so that the person taking the sounding could report the seabed conditions to his superior, such as: solid or soft, sand or mud, gritty or rocky. This meant that these conditions could be given, at any point, as the ship was manoeuvred.

Spick and Span. (Clean and tidy, looking good)

'Spick' is another word for 'Spike', and 'Span', another word for 'Chip'. Both words were used to describe a brand new ship, just launched, and possibly out of the dock for the first time. She would be showing shiny new-metal, and fresh-wood 'chips', which would still be littered-about, her un-trodden decks.

Spin a yarn. (The telling of a tall story, or a convincing lie)

This saying originated around the early 1800s (1810 was the first recorded usage) and refers to rope making, which was usually carried out by seamen, working in pairs, when there was little of other-employment, needing to be carried out, aboard the ship.

The 'Spinners' would tell stories as they worked on this boring-type of activity. Having spent months, or years, at sea, sailors would have interesting tales to tell about their experiences. (Mostly exaggerated, romanticised, or downright fictitious.) These yarns would be told while working on small jobs, such as splicing short ends of rope (See 'Fag ends') into smaller, more serviceable items, e.g. 'stopping', (used for 'caulking') or 'yarn', to make the furling of sails to the yards, easier; shorter pieces could be used for splicing into thinner pieces of ropes. They were even used for making soft toys. The threads in a rope, or pieces of cordage, are also called 'Yarn'. (See 'Junk')

Splice the main brace. (Take a drink after hard work)
In the days of sail, particularity in bad weather, the 'splicing of the main brace' was, physically, an extremely difficult task to perform, due to its location: it being attached to the main lower-yard. At a calculated guess, it could be said that after this difficult task had been performed, especially in bad weather, the men involved would be ready for a drink, and be given an extra tot of rum. (See 'Grog')

Sprog. (Slang for a child, or a raw recruit.)
This is a slang word, used in most of the armed services, including the navy, so it is not an exclusive maritime expression; although it has been rumoured that it orig-

inated from a maritime source, there seems to be no proof of this. It could, possibly, have derived from the word 'Sprocket', (small cog in a big wheel.) Another name given to a child, or a new recruit, would be 'Shaver' (nicknamed so, because they were too young to shave).

Square meal. (A substantial and satisfying meal)
This dates back many hundreds of years, when the quality of food aboard ship was poor. It is a nautical expression meaning any significant meal, served on board, at a time when food was dished up on large square wooden trays. As living space was limited, the seamen would take their food back to their posts and consume it whilst on duty. These square wooden plates, or trays, were designed so that they could be easily stored. Some believe that a 'Square meal' is a seaman's biscuit, known as, 'Hard tack', which was also square and would often be infested with weevils. (See also 'Slush fund')

Square up. (To settle an account. To face and tackle someone, or something)
The bosun, or the officer in charge, would check all sails, when the ship was in dock or in harbour, making absolutely sure they were safely squared up, and correctly tied off.

Squeegee. (A rubber edged broom)
Originally, this maritime word was 'Squilgee', which was a swab used for cleaning the ship's decks. It was a

colloquialism for, 'Squeeze' or 'Squeegee'. It is also a cam-shaped tool, used for shaping frames on the 'Bending slab'

Standing. (High-status position. Esteem. Upright)
A vessel is, 'brought up all standing', when there is no time to lower sails, i.e. when forced to slow very quickly, because sails have been put 'Aback' by a sudden change of wind. (See 'Aback')

Staunch. (Strong and reliable)
A vessel that is well built and reliable, being sturdy, strong and free from leaks.

Stem the tide. (To prevent, resist, stop something detrimental happening)
The 'Stem' consists of the forward-most pieces of timber in the ship's keel, which joins the bows of the ship at the lower end of the keel; the bowsprit is attached to the upper end of the stem. When a ship's keel lies too flat, not allowing her to ride the wind in the correct manner, it would be difficult to 'Make way'. The stem of the keel would then be said to be, 'stemming the tide'. Colloquially, it means to resist being overtaken by undesirable happenings.

Stick an oar in. (To meddle or cause trouble by interfering, or to stir things up) (See 'Oars')

Strop, or Stroppy. **(Irritable, bad tempered, difficult to deal with)**
A collar of leather, spliced rope, or iron, to surround a block, which is used for handling cargo. This 'strop' is required to take considerable strain. 'In a strop,' colloquially, means to be under great strain, to become irritable or angry.

Sweet F.A. ('Sweet Fanny Adams', meaning: of no consequence)
Back in 1867, a young girl called 'Fanny Adams', who lived at Alton in Hampshire, was brutally murdered at just eight years of age. Around that period, came the first issue of tinned meat to the navy. The unimpressed sailors were reputed to have said that it was the remains of 'Fanny Adams'. The name then became synonymous with stewed meat or mutton, now considered to mean 'nothing', or not of any relevance.

Swinging a cat (See 'No room to swing a cat')

Swinging the lead. (Avoiding hard work, or playing 'Hookey')
In the early days of sail, when there was little work to do, a sailor might be given the job of sitting on the 'Cathead', (the horizontal beam where the anchor might hang) on the ship's forward quarter, holding a lead-weighted line over the side of the ship. This would be used to establish the depth of water, below the ship, to ensure that there was no likelihood of the vessel running aground. The rope would have 'ties'

placed at measured intervals, i.e. a fathom, or six feet apart. The bottom end of the weight would have been dipped in tallow or fat. When it touched bottom, the 'Linesman', who was, 'swinging the lead', would haul the weight inboard, counting the markers as he did so; he would then shout out the result to the Captain, mate, or steersman, advising them of the depth; and by studying the state of the tallow or fat, he could judge the state of the ground below, i.e. if it was rocky or sandy. Colloquially, 'Swinging the lead' means, to avoid hard work, or dodging work, which in this case, would be seen, by shipmates, as an easy job. (See also 'Fathom' and 'Hooky')

Tack. (A chosen course or to change direction according to progress)

'Tack' was an abbreviation of 'Hard Tack' (See also 'Square meal'), which is a ship's hard biscuit. As a nautical expression, it means sailing a 'Zigzag' course, taking advantage of any available wind by changing direction. 'Tacking into the wind' was a favourable way for a ship to make progress, to make some 'headway'. (See 'Headway') As a colloquialism, it means that matters might be best resolved, by changing direction.

Take down a peg or two. (To deflate a person's ego)

A ship's colours were usually secured to the 'Halyards' by 'Toggles', similar to those found on duffel coats. Pegs were used to raise or lower these colours. The higher up the rigging they were sited, after completion of a successful battle, the greater the honour bestowed to the ship and crew. To take down, or lower this position, would diminish the honour. On a warship, where rigging had been destroyed, the crew would nail her colours as high up the main mast as possible, when even greater honours would be gained. (See 'Nailing colours to the mast')

Taken aback. (Shock or surprise, or to be disconcerted by a sudden action)
This is a nautical term for a sudden wind-change, when the sails get flattened against the masts, especially in the face of unexpected strong-winds. In the case of a 'Square rigged' ship, such a wind could halt the ship from any forward movement, and could even cause the vessel to be driven backwards. The ship would then be referred to as being: 'Taken-Aback'. (See also 'Aback' and Figure 01)

Take the wind out of one's sails. (A Surprise, or sudden shock, that has an overpowering effect)
In early sea-battle days, when sails were the only means of propulsion, a ship would pass, as close as it dared, to an enemy ship, in order to put it on the windward side. This would block the wind from the enemy vessel and cause it to 'lose way'. This would be of great advantage, as the enemy ship would then become virtually motionless, and so become a sitting target for canon fire. (See also 'Make way')

Tampon. (A plug of soft, absorbent material)
A variation of the word 'Tampion', also 'Tapon', which is an ornamental wooden-plug, or stopper, to protect the open barrel of a gun, or canon. A type of 'Tampon' was also used to stem bleeding from wounds; these were made of soft material, or smooth wood, wrapped in cloth, and placed into the wound, before it was bound, in order to slow or to stop the flow of blood.

Thimble. (A finger protection, used when hand-sewing)
A pear-shaped iron-ring, with a curved outer-surface, into which a rope would sit, so that splicing could take place around it. It was also used as protection, in order to prevent ropes from becoming tangled; and to add strength to a rope, when a hook or metal tackle was passed through, or around it. (*See Figure 21*)

THIMBLE

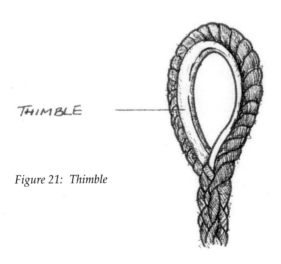

Figure 21: Thimble

Three sheets to the wind. (Someone unsteady, usually due to excess of alcohol)
Derived from the fact, that if a ship's sails were loose or incorrectly raised, the vessel would roll unsteadily about; and if the ship's sheets (control ropes) were flying free, the ship would be difficult to steer. Colloquially, it refers to a person who is the worse for wear, due to over indulgence of alcohol, and so, rendered incapable.

Through the hoop. (Punishment)
In the early days of sail, especially on warships, space was at a premium. Each member of the crew, *'below decks'*, would only be entitled to bring aboard a few personal possessions; these would have to be made into a certain shape and size, so that the bundle would pass through a specially made hoop, which the bosun would hold. If the parcel was too large, the poor sailor would be given a blow with the bosun's knotted rope. *'Put through the hoop'*, also applied to hammocks, which would have to be folded and rolled again, into the correct size. The crew of a 'Man-o-war', needed to line the inside of the ships' keel with their bedding; this helped to protect them, and their ship, from any penetration of the enemy's canon fire. (*See 'Grasp the nettle'*)

Tide over. (To make do with whatever is available, over an awkward or difficult period of time, especially financially, until matters improve)
Sailing ships, 'beating' down the English Channel against a head wind, would not always be in a position

to 'Make way', against such weather. (See 'Tack') In these conditions, outward-bound shipping-vessels could make little progress; and would often seek to 'rest up', or even to anchor in a safe harbour, while tides and winds were against them. (See also 'Any port in a storm' and 'Make way')

Toe the line. (To obey orders, conform to a general policy or principal)
On board ship, at 'Muster', (Roll call) orders would come to: 'Beat to quarters' or 'Divisions' (meaning to report for duty or to go below to the beating of a drum). The crew would be expected to parade on time, and to line themselves up, with toes touching one of the decking planks - so that they were ready for inspection. (See also 'Show' or 'Shake a leg.')

Tot. (A small measure of drink, or a small child)
'Tot-time,' in the British navy, was usually given out at 11.15.am, for those on afternoon watch, and at 12.00.mid-day for the rest of the non-commissioned members of the ship's company. Commissioned Officers, of course, would serve themselves. The 'tot' amounted to a half gill of spirit for each crewmember. Now a day, they have to accept two or three cans of beer, as consolation for losing the 'Tot'.

Touch and go. (A near miss)
Nautically, it refers to: almost running a vessel aground, accidentally, but just managing to re-float the ship, in the nick of time, before she actually does run

aground. Metaphorically, it means a narrow escape, or circumstances that one is lucky to escape from.

Trim one's sails. (To make changes, according to circumstances or situations)
'Trimming the sails,' happens on board ship, when there is need for a change of direction. And also to keeping the vessel neat and tidy - looking good when sailing under canvas. (See also 'Plane sailing')

Truck. ('To have no truck with' meaning: to avoid dealing with someone or something)
A 'Truck', in maritime terms, is a circular, wheel-shaped metal ring, used to lift the spars and crosstrees up the masts, before the sails were fixed. The 'Truck' would stop short of the mast top, under the 'Button'. A Truck is also a small-wheeled trolley, used to move canons around the gun decks. This term has been used for centuries, but in modern day language it refers to a vehicle carrying heavy loads. (See also 'Nailing your colours to the mast' and 'Button')

Turn a blind eye. (Under the weather, indisposed, out of sorts, feeling ill) (See 'Blind eye')
If a seaman got hurt or taken ill, whilst at sea, he would be sent, if possible, below or between decks, to recover. Under, or between decks, was considered to be out of harm's way, and underneath any bad weather, which would, supposedly, allow him to recover his health and strength.

Union Jack. (British national flag)

In the Royal Navy, whenever the British national flag is flown at sea, it is called, 'The Union Jack'. (Jack being sailor) When flown on land, however, it is called, 'The Union Flag'. The Royal Navy always flies the 'White Ensign' flag, which has the 'Red Cross' of St George, on a white background, with the Union Jack taking up the top quarter of the 'Red Cross', (nearest to the hanging point) known by seafarers as, 'The white duster'. The merchant navy flies a red flag, which has the Union Jack in a similar position. (Known as the 'Red duster'). Occasionally, one sees the Union flag being flown wrongly, by mistake, in an upside down position, which should only be done as a, 'Sign of distress'; otherwise, the wider, white diagonal-band, on the Union flag, should always be shown at the top of the flag, when adjacent to the flagpole or hanging point. (See Figure 22)

Figure 22:
Union Jack/Union Flag

Up the pole. (To be crazy or eccentric)
Ships' masts were sometimes referred to as 'Poles', especially the sections above the rigging, which were considered to be in a most precarious and dangerous place. (See 'Shrouds' and 'Stays') Anyone taking leave of their senses, by ignoring safety-rules, when climbing a pole, (which sometimes happened when showing off) was considered to be a bit of a lunatic, and said to be 'Up the pole'. A false move, in this situation, would very likely end in disaster.

Wad. (A number of bank notes, rolled or placed together)
A plug of rolled wadding, rope, or soft wood, used for ramming or forcing down the muzzle of a musket or gun, in order to keep the powder tight, and ready for firing. It also helped to keep the powder dry, and in place, which could enhance the propulsion of the shot, as it was being fired. (See also 'Tampon')

Waister / Waster. (Idle, wasteful person)
In naval terms, an unskilled labourer, usually employed in the 'waist' of a ship, who would be used for carrying out menial and unskilled tasks, such as hauling ropes or disposing of the ship's waste. It is possible that the term would have been used for new and inexperienced seamen, when they were still considered 'Landlubbers'.

Wallop. (An alcoholic drink, usually, strong beer, or a heavy blow)

In the 16th century, the French navy attacked, and sacked, the south coast town of Brighton. King Henry the eighth then instructed Admiral Wallop to attack the French, in order to teach them a lesson. After creating havoc all along the French coast, it was said he gave the French: *'an awful walloping'*. (Thrashing) On their return to England, copious amounts of alcohol were consumed, and widespread drunkenness followed; hence the call for: *'A drop of Wallop'*.

Weather eye. (Keeping a keen lookout)

A person on guard, whose job it is to keep a watch-out for squally or bad weather, is called, 'The Weather eye' It also refers to making sure that everything is going well, and is usually the job of the 'Top man', or lookout.

Weather the storm. (Survive the best way one can, through difficult conditions that are beyond one's control)

In heavy weather, if a vessel is unlikely to make safe harbour, in order to gain protection from a pending storm, the captain, most certainly, would minimize the dangers, by issuing certain orders, e.g. that all hatches and loose deck-items be made secure, that all sails be made ready for storm conditions etc. In other words, to be prepared in every possible way, in order to, 'ride-out' or 'weather the storm'; with every effort to minimize damage to the ship and crew.

Wending/winding. (Making one's way)
Swinging a ship's head (or bows) around, to an oppos-
ing direction. Turning with the tide, in order to change
course.

**Wet (or Whet). (To, 'wet one's whistle', to have a
drink)**
When ashore, in overcrowded pubs and clubs, some
sailors carried a whistle to attract the attention of the
landlord or the serving wench, in order to get a drink.
Some even had a whistle soldered to the tankard's handle. The alternative meant, pushing their way to the
overcrowded bar, where it was often impossible to be
served; they would then be told to, "go and whistle for
it."

**Whale of a time. (A hectic, frivolous partying, a
greatly enjoyable time)**
Of maritime origin, (some would call it: 'A wail of a
time') meaning: jollities, with much shrieking and
laughing, or fun and games. It relates to the whale, the
largest, living mammal, which even dwarfs the ele-
phant. The blue whale grows to over 30 metres in
length, and weighs in at some 150 tonnes. Therefore, a
whale of this size, frolicking, darting and diving,
would be a huge and demonstrative rollicking-affair.

**When my ship comes in. (Waiting for something
good to happen, or wealth to be forthcoming)**
Merchants would put up funds for the use and hire of
trading vessels that were travelling abroad, so that they
would bring home for them, on the return journey,

many exotic cargoes, from abroad. These merchants would wait, nervously, for the ship's safe return, with their valuable cargoes in good order. With this achieved, they could maximise on their investments. So the phrase is synonymous with making a fortune. (See also 'On the nail')

Whistle for it. (See whet, or wet your whistle)

Wide berth. (To keep clear of danger, give enough space around a difficult situation, or person)
The saying: 'to give a wide berth to', dates back to the heyday of sail, in the 17th century. Then, it meant: 'a place where there is sea room to moor a ship'. Later, 'berth' became more widely used as meaning: 'distance from'. Colloquially, 'to give a wide berth to', is taken as advise to keep clear of impending problems.

Wild goose-chase. (Foolish, or hopeless, unproductive quest)
The origin of this saying is obscure, although some would believe that it refers to the native American Indians, of the 'Wild Goose Nations', where it was said: that when they saw the white sails of ships, they would refer to them as wild geese sailing over the ocean, and were therefore impossible to chase or to capture. As far as is known, there is no officially recognized origin.

THE END

The Topsail Schooner
'Kathleen & May' (1900)
Brunswick Wharf, Bideford, Devon

Should readers know of any further maritime words or sayings, and can include their origins and reference, please advise me either by email to:
tj.parker@tiscali.co.uk

or via the internet on:
www.heartsofoak.net

or telephone me on:
(01271) 374286.

This may help with any further issues, or reprints of this book. If used, the entry will be accredited to the sender.

Acknowledgements

Special thanks to writer and poet Joyce Moon for helping me to break down technical explanations and for helping me to translate the book's contents into everyday language.

Thanks also go to Gary Carter of Braunton, who kindly drew up the figured drawings for me, some of which were re-arranged from details found elsewhere.

Cover drawing was kindly donated by
Kate Sisley-Rayner BA(hons)
Now living in Scotland

Grateful thanks are also offered to the many knowledgeable people, too many to list, consulted on this book's content.

Profits from this publication will be given to maritime charities.

References

Confirmation of many listed entries has been researched, and opinions have been considered from the following publications:

Shanties and sailor songs. Stan Hugill
                              pub. Herbert Jenkins,
                                          London.

Shanties from the seven seas. Stan Hugill
                              pub. Routeledge and Kegan Paul
                                                          Ltd.

The Country Life Book of Nautical Terms.
                              pub. Country Life Books

Ship to Shore   Peter D. Dean
                                  pub. ABC-Clio

Jackspeak   Rick Jolly
                                  British Library,
                              Admiral W.H. Smyth
                          pub. Conway Maritime Press.

A sea of words   Dean King
                              An owl book, Henry Holt
                              with John Hattendorf,
                                  pub. J. Worth Estes.

INDEX

Buttock
Button
Bye-bye, (Bi-Bi)
By and large

C
Carry the can
Catch a packet
Catwalk
Chantey
Chewing the fat
Choc-a-block
Chop-chop
Clean bill of health
Clean slate
Clean sweep
Clear as a bell
Clear the decks
Clewed (Clued) up
Close to the wind
Coast is clear
Cocked hat
Cock-up
Collar
Copper-bottomed
Corker
Couple of shakes
Crack-on
Craft
Crimp
Crossing the line

Cut and run
Cut of his jib

D
Dab hand
Dead in the water
Dead on time
Dead reckoning
Dead wood
Derrick
Deserting a sinking ship
Devil to pay
Dip out
Doesn't cut much ice
Dog's body
Doldrums
Donkey's breakfast
Donkey work
Dressing down

E
Earmarked
Earring
Eat one's hat
Edge away

F
Fag end
Fagged out
Fair enough
Fall foul

Fathom
Feeling blue
Fend off
Fiddle
Field-day
Figurehead
Fill one's boots
First-rate
Flake out
Flash in the pan
Flogging a dead horse
Fluke
Fly-by-night
Flyer
Flying colours
Frisby
Full-flood

G
Gaff
Gingerbread
Give someone the slip
Glad rags
Glory-hole
Go ahead
Go by the board
Grasp the nettle
Grog or Groggy
Guff

H
Half-cocked
Hand over fist
Hang fire
Hard and fast
Hard up
Headway
Heavy weather
Heckle
High and dry
Hijack
Hold on too long
Hooky or Hoaky
Hot shot
Hunky-dory

I / J
Ill wind
Jack knife
Jerry built
Jump ship
Junk

K
Keel over
Knots
Knowing the ropes

L
Laid-up
Lanyard
Lash up
Learning the ropes
Let fly
Let the cat out of
    the bag
Limelight
Listless
Logbook
Loggerheads
Long shot
Loom
Loop-holes
Loose cannon
Loose ends
Lump sum

M
Mainstay
Make and mend
Make way
Making a rod for
    your own back.
Match
Mate
Maul
Mayday
Mayonnaise
Miss the boat
Money for old rope

Moonlighting
My eye

N
Nailing one's colours
    to the mast
Nautical
Nipper
Nitty-gritty
No great shakes
No room to swing a cat
Nous

O
Oars
Odds and sods
Off the wall
Oil on troubled waters
Old man
Oldster
On an even keel
On the beach
On the nail
On strike
Out of the blue
Out on a limb
Over a barrel
Overboard
Overhaul
Overwhelmed

P

Packet
Parting shot
Paunch
Pickled
Pigeon holed
Pillar to post
Pinch
Piping hot
Plane (Plain) sailing
Plumb the depths
Plumb-line
Pooped
Posh
Pram
Put about

Q

Quarantine
Quid

R

Rack and ruin
Rate of knots
Rest on your oars
Ringleader
Round Robin
Rover
Rule of thumb

S

Sail under false
  colours
Salt
Scandalize
Scrambled egg
Scraper
Scraping the barrel
Scratch my back
Scrub 'round it
Seize
Sewn up
Shake (or show)
  a leg
Shakes
Shanty
Shape up
Sheets
Shipshape
Shivers
Shove off
Shrouds
Sideboards
Sideburns
Skyscraper
Slackers
Slip
Slush fund
Snotty
Sod's law
Son of a gun
Soundings
Spick and span

Spin a yarn
Splice the mainbrace
Sprog
Square meal
Square up
Squeegee
Standing
Staunch
Stem the tide
Stick an oar in
Strop or Stroppy
Sweet F.A.
Swing a cat
Swing the lead

T
Tack
Take down a peg
Taken aback
Take the wind out
  of ones sails
Tampon / Tampion
Thimble
Three sheets to
  the wind
Through the hoop
Tide over
Toe the line
Tot
Touch and go
Trim one's sails

Truck
Turn a blind eye

U
Under the weather
Union Jack
Up the pole

V / W
Wad
Waister (Waster)
Wallop
Weather eye
Weather the storm
Wending
Wet (Whet)
Whale of a time
"When one's ship comes in"
Whistle for it
Wide berth
Wild goose chase

Reader's Notes

Reader's Notes

Reader's Notes

Reader's Notes

Reader's Notes

Reader's Notes

Reader's Notes